ESSENCE OF
ESG

A PRACTITIONER'S PERSPECTIVE

ESSENCE OF ESG

A PRACTITIONER'S PERSPECTIVE

VIPUL ARORA

Worldwide Published by
Pendown Press

PENDOWN PRESS LLP

An ISO 9001 & ISO 14001 Certified Co.,

Regd. Office: 3767A, Kanhaiya Nagar,

Tri Nagar, Delhi-110035

Ph.: 8130886000, 9650072927, 8595249536

E-mail: info@pendownpress.com

Branch Office: 1A/2A, 20, Hari Sadan, Ansari Road,

Daryaganj, New Delhi-110002

Ph.: 011-45794768

Website: PendownPress.com

First Edition: 2024

ISBN: 978-93-5554-854-2

Layout and Cover Designed by Pendown Graphics Team
Printed and Bound in India by Thomson Press India Ltd.

Dedication

This book is dedicated to...

YOU!

and all those who will work on ESG, continuing to make its promise a reality.

Also, to all my friends and colleagues who have been leading the growth of ESG and Sustainability over the years, despite various obstacles.

Contents

About the Author

Vipul started his adventure in Sustainability more than 25 years ago, at a time when it was not much heard of. He tried to implement Sustainability in the Corporate and NGO sector from 1997 to 2007. Later, he pioneered ESG Ratings and research in 15 Emerging markets in 2007. He has worked on most of the leading ESG rating methodologies to assess over 10,000+ companies globally across 69 sectors. He created an award-winning Emerging market focused ESG rating methodology in 2010, which gained the trust of major global investors managing more than $13 Trillion of investments. He was selected as a fellow at Stanford University twice. His professional journey has spanned various roles within ESG Rating agencies, Corporations, NGOs, collaboration with Government agencies, and Consultancies, taking him from India to the US, Europe, UK, UAE, Mexico, Brazil and Chile. Vipul has been a speaker at 50+ global industry conferences on ESG.

In 2018, he was recognized as one of the top 25 people globally who have made the most positive contribution to ESG. Vipul currently serves as Partner, ESG & Climate Solutions at Sattva Consulting **(www.sattva.co.in).** All views expressed in this book are personal.

> "First, they ignore you, then they laugh at you,
> then they fight you, then you win."
> - *Mahatma Gandhi*

ESG has been going through a similar journey.

ESG, Sustainable development, and Climate change represent the greatest disruption in 300 years of Industrial history.

Companies and Industries will either transform or disappear.

Who is this book for?

For anyone who wants to understand ESG better...

...especially for beginners.

Praise for this Book

"In a world increasingly full of 'ESG pretenders' and 'instant converts', Vipul is the genuine article, and is therefore eminently worth listening to. He has been a pioneer and innovator in the field, particularly in the critical area of emerging markets since 2007. Here he has written a valuable and extremely timely introduction to ESG, one which will undoubtedly create, educate, and encourage a whole new generation of committed practitioners. He has done us all a service."

Dr. Matthew Kiernan, Founder, Innovest (now MSCI ESG). Innovest was one of the co-authors of the report "Who cares wins" along with UNEP-FI that coined the term 'ESG' in 2004.

"It takes deep understanding, mastery, and experience to simplify and boil things down to their essence. That is precisely what Vipul has done with 'Essence of ESG'—a true gem of a book. He tells you everything you need to know about the burgeoning ESG industry—and why you should care."

Dr. Stuart L. Hart, Professor and author of 'Capitalism at the Crossroads'. One of the founding fathers of the Corporate Sustainability movement in the US since 1970's.

"I have known Vipul since his EM ESG startup Solaron joined PRI in 2010. At a time when ESG was gaining traction in mature markets, it was almost non-existent in emerging markets, and Vipul was well ahead of his time. In this book, Vipul seeks to expand ESG education and drive its adoption further into emerging markets......"

Dr. James Gifford, Head of Sustainable & Impact Advisory & Thought Leadership, Credit Suisse. Founding Executive Director & CEO 2003 — 2013 of the UN Principles for Responsible Investment (UN PRI).

"ESG has a long, rich, vibrant, and impactful history. It continues to evolve globally, encompassing a variety of philosophies, approaches, intentions, and outcomes.

It takes someone with a deep understanding of, and experience in ESG to communicate not just the key highlights of ESG's growth and success, but the potential it holds to empower investors in the future.

Vipul's three decades of ESG leadership informs his perspectives and insights, which he has generously shared in the 'Essence of ESG'. Reading this book is time well spent – for those exploring ESG for the first time and long-time ESG practitioners alike."

Michael Jantzi, Founder, Sustainalytics (now Morningstar), Board Member, International Sustainability Standards Board (ISSB)

"Vipul was years ahead of his time when he began work in Sustainability in 1997 and on ESG in 2007 by starting Solaron, the pioneering EM ESG research and rating firm. Sustainability and ESG were not popular in those days, as they are now. He committed to this as a career, due to his conviction and passion for it. This is what convinced me and fellow Investors to support Solaron in their early years.

In this book, Vipul has condensed his years of experience into a simple and easy to understand manual on ESG that will be a useful companion for anyone who wants to begin their career in ESG and Climate. Vipul is a true inspiration as he persevered on his vision over the years that made him an authority on this subject, as ESG has become mandatory now."

Nagaraja Prakasam, Co-founder IAN (Indian Angels Network) Impact, Angel Investor, Mentor, Fund Advisor, and Author of the book: "Back to Bharat — In search of a sustainable future."

"It gives me great pleasure to recommend Vipul's new book on ESG. Concise, simple, and to the point, "Essence of ESG" is the perfect guidebook for those who want to catch up and learn the practical concepts of merging sustainability principles in their work.

My journey with Vipul started more than 18 years ago. Back then, sustainability was gaining solid traction in western financial markets, but had little if any penetration in emerging markets.

I was then Managing Director at Innovest in San Francisco and was looking for ways to scale and streamline our ESG research operations, when I first met Vipul. With his natural good-hearted idealism and boundless enthusiasm, he was looking for his next challenge in pushing the frontier of sustainability further. And so, I had the privilege of enlisting Vipul's help in starting a research center in Bangalore India, for our firm Innovest Strategic Value Advisors.

I trained Vipul and his newly recruited team of 15 researchers in the science of ESG research, scoring and rating. The operation was a success, but when Innovest got acquired in 2009 by RiskMetrics (later MSCI), Vipul had to pivot his ESG research operation and find a new challenge. That's how he created "Best in Context" rating model, a novel and brilliant framework for rating companies in emerging countries with a multinational team of researchers in 15 emerging countries: ESG with ears-on-the-ground as it were! I consider Vipul to be a real innovator in ESG research and a tested entrepreneur.

Warning: "Vipul's passion for making the world a better place is contagious. Reader beware!"

Pierre Trevet, 25 years in sustainable investment innovation, Founder and CEO of Helios Exchange, Inc.

Why this Book?

Global need

Our world is dealing with many multidimensional problems, both local and global. These problems cover climate change, pollution, loss of biodiversity, poverty, human rights, workers' rights, bribery, corruption, migration, unequal growth and development, to name a few. These issues cannot be solved in isolation. We need multiple stakeholders to work together. ESG provides the necessary framework to enable this collaboration.

Those who offer solutions to these pressing challenges have the potential to participate in a remarkable $40 Trillion worth of new business opportunities. However, these solutions cannot be created in the background of talent shortages and knowledge gaps, which are prevalent at this moment. There is a need to share ESG knowledge and skills with as many people as possible - a goal this book aims to achieve.

Personal contribution

During my journey in ESG and Sustainability, I was fortunate to receive the right support and guidance at crucial moments. I want to share with you, what I have received. This is one of the driving forces behind this book.

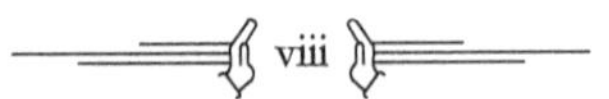

ESG is a multidimensional topic. In the early years, I faced difficulty explaining my work to family and friends. I have tried to overcome this challenge by using simple language and examples in this book that everyone can understand. It is my intention to eliminate barriers for beginners, making ESG more accessible and relatable for you. If you find the language of this book too simple, it means I have succeeded in achieving my purpose. If not, please let me know, and I would be happy to make improvements.

For a person who is sincere and can apply the ESG concepts well in creating practical solutions, a career in ESG has the potential to bring above average income and a high growth, long-term career. Equally, it brings the fulfilment of making a positive impact on nature, our living environment, employees, customers, and the community.

High Growth + Positive Impact together!
This is priceless!

If you use the principles shared in this book well, you would be able to achieve success in applying ESG in your life and work. It would bring me immense joy to witness your success in ESG.

How Can this Book Help You?

This book will:

- Explain ESG and its application in a simple language.

- It will help you learn quickly and efficiently, the most important aspects of ESG.

- If you reflect on the contents of this book, it will support you to confidently apply the concepts of ESG in your role, leaving doubt, uncertainty, and hesitation behind.

- Help you achieve success through ESG in your role and organization.

How to Get the Best Value From this Book?

Please read it with an Open and Curious mind.

This book is NOT for you:

1. If you think what you are doing is already perfect and there is no room for further improvement.

2. If you are going to read it while constantly judging it, comparing it with other books or if you are distracted while reading it.

You simply will not get value from it.

Here, I share what I have observed, learned, reflected upon, and lived during 25 years of practice. I started working on Sustainability initially and later delved into ESG when not many knew or cared about these terms. I commenced this journey in 1997, a time when internet access was limited, emails were not used universally, and neither was the mobile phone accessible to all; social media did not even exist. Starting in that era, I have kept going in my search and inquiry. I was not chasing a lucrative career. I have cared about sustainability and ESG for so long that I've persisted all these years. I love what I do; it doesn't feel like work at all.

My search was never theoretical. My learnings derive from lived experience. I always sought to practice what I was learning, to the best of my abilities. I tried to implement specific and relevant aspects of Sustainability into all my roles during my career. Once I was absolutely certain, I started a company to offer ESG Ratings and research. I am not perfect, but I tried to implement what I was learning in my work. I made a lot of mistakes. These mistakes taught me much more than my successes did.

However, despite that, feel free to accept what resonates with you. Use it and experiment with it. If it delivers results, adopt it. If it doesn't deliver the desired results, let's have a discussion. There are a lot of nuances in implementation. And comprehending something new in depth is the first step to success. Executing it without any doubts or inhibitions marks the second step. Only then can we get the full result. So, before you assess whether these insights are working for you or not, ask yourself if you've passed this two-step test.

Besides, Sustainability and ESG require a lot of patience. You can see Sustainability only when it's not there. If it is missing, it is very easy to see that it is absent. This is the nature of sustainability.

Recall the words of Thomas Edison: "I have not failed 10,000 times—I've successfully found 10,000 ways that will not work".

This is true for all scientific research and discovery. It's even more relevant in the realm of Sustainability and ESG, considering that the problems we strive to solve are multi-dimensional and involve multiple stakeholders. It is quite a challenge. So, should we despair and give up? No.

What is the way to determine if you are succeeding in implementing Sustainability and ESG?

There is a simple mantra: 'If, as a result of your efforts, all stakeholders, including yourself, are happy and satisfied, it is sustainable. If this is not true yet, keep working, keep iterating. Don't give up.' I can assure you that success in applying ESG is possible. In fact, the results will be far better, more durable, and much more fulfilling.

I wish that your ESG journey benefits from mine - so that you don't have to face the same challenges and obstacles that I faced.

Let's begin!

– Yours Truly.

Chapter 1

Essence of ESG

ESG stands for Environmental, Social and Corporate Governance. It serves as a lens, a perspective, a new framework for assessing companies based on their Environmental, Social and Corporate Governance performance, moving beyond the traditional financial performance lens.

Why should you care about ESG?

ESG is a powerful trend that is shaping the 21st century.

Institutional Investors that manage over 60% of Global Investments (approx. USD 120 Trillion) have committed to using ESG as an additional factor in their research.

ESG encourages companies, investors and stock markets to go beyond their obsession with the short-term value of their stock prices and focus on creating long-term value. This shift opens up new possibilities for Companies to generate transformational value for both people and the planet, all while making profits.

Climate change is one of the various themes covered within ESG, among many others.

ESG and climate change demands from clients, investors and regulators are changing the rules of the game for everyone. No one will be left untouched. Whether you are a business or an individual, you can no longer ignore ESG. It has become necessary to prepare for the future.

The ESG-led transformation is going to create opportunities worth $40 Trillion, equal to the combined GDP of two of the largest economies: the USA and China. Most Large companies have already recognized the importance of ESG and have initiated a race to secure the biggest share of this pie. The proof? While the technology industry is declining, ESG is booming.

In 2022, 135,000 employees in the IT sector lost their jobs globally. On the other hand, there are 300,000 open jobs in the ESG sector globally, waiting to be filled.

During the same year, employers worldwide offered 2.4 million ESG jobs. This number is expected to increase to 24 million jobs by 2030 – that is 10 times, in just 7 years!

However, 2030 is too far. Currently, most people in the ESG field already have multiple job offers in hand, offering higher salaries and elevated roles. The demand for ESG talent is already far greater than the supply.

Many companies are exponentially increasing their exposure to ESG products and services, especially in areas like ESG reporting, benchmarking, SDG's, Carbon and climate change, net-zero goals and targets. As a result, the demand for ESG skilled talent will remain high for the next several decades.

If you are a job seeker, it is worth investing in your career growth by starting to learn about ESG and building capacity, ensuring you remain a leader in your organization. Don't wait for a crisis to upskill, switch roles or careers. True leaders always stay ahead of their time, anticipating new trends and being prepared when opportunity arises at their doorstep.

If you are a job creator, you are either already reporting on the ESG reporting requirements in multiple jurisdictions or preparing to report on them. Multiple Regulatory requirements or Client mandates are already asking you to prepare your ESG reports and demonstrate how you are integrating them better than the competition.

Hence, this is a good moment to evaluate: Where are you on your ESG journey?

The earlier you start your ESG journey, the greater the opportunities that will become available to you.

Further Details on ESG

ESG is simply a research and analysis framework that drills down into the parameters of Environmental, Social and Corporate

Governance within any organization. When you combine the initial letters of these three terms and make an acronym, you get ESG.

This section is set up as a conversation you are having with your friend or colleague on ESG.

Question: OK, so what does ESG stand for?

Answer: Well, ESG represents the 3 pillars or dimensions of a company's performance: Environmental, Social and Corporate Governance. These dimensions of a company are at least as important as financial performance. ESG is a framework that allows us to assess the performance of an organizational unit or a company from the specific point of view of ESG criteria.

Question: Why, so?

Answer: Because what the company does in these 3 areas today is going to reflect in its financial numbers later on.

Question: How?

Answer: To understand this, let's delve into each of these three areas, shall we?

Question: Yes, go on. So, what does 'E' represent?

Answer: The E or the Environmental pillar encompasses all the interactions the company has with its natural environment. Consider that any company, in order to manufacture its products or offer services, needs to consume natural resources. For example, how much energy is the company using? What about its consumption of raw materials, water, fuels, land resources? Is the company highly efficient in using these resources? Or is there room for improvement?

The environmental pillar, therefore, includes all the input and output interactions the company is having with its natural environment. Some examples: raw materials used, waste created, the effect of that waste on the natural environment (e.g., greenhouse gases leading to climate change), impact on biodiversity, water usage and waste water production, energy efficiency, etc.

We are most interested in those interactions that affect its financial performance. Such interactions are called 'material' interactions. 'Material' interactions or 'Materiality' implies anything that can have a potential financial impact.

Question: But how does this matter?

Answer: Well, all these resources come at a cost, don't they? So, if a company is using them efficiently and not wasting them, it will save costs and increase profits, right?

Question: Yes, but are not some of the resources free?

Answer: Maybe some of them are. For example, a company may have access to free fresh water at some facility, but how long is it going to remain free? Forever? No!

So, it is better for the company to consider its natural resource consumption and seek efficiency in using them. We DO NOT have an unlimited amount of natural resources on this planet!

It was already said in the 1990s that humanity was using more resources than the earth can provide. This research is known as 'foot printing'. Scientists conducted resource foot printing and reported in the earlier 1990s itself that we had started to use far more resources than the earth can sustain. Hence, we need to reduce the speed at which we are depleting the earth's resources.

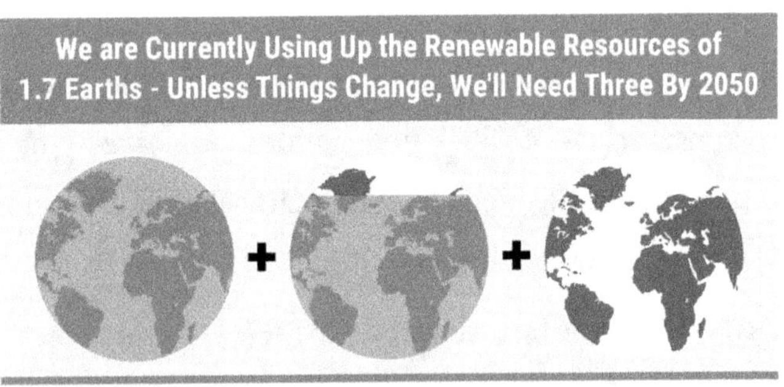

Figure 1: Running out of Natural resources

1# **Source:** Global Footprint Network; under CC BY-SA 4.0 DEED Attribution-ShareAlike 4.0 International

Question: How will that help?

Answer: Well, the Earth and nature in general have the capacity to replenish their resources, which we refer to as, natural resources. However, they do so at a certain pace due to the cycles in nature.

Now, if we consume any resource at a rate faster than nature can replenish, we will eventually run out of it, leading to a shortage, right?

Question: Yes, but what does it have to do with the company and its financial performance?

Answer: Well, at the beginning of the industrial revolution in the late - 18th century, it was assumed that we could use any amount of water in factories or any amount of land to do agriculture, and extract unlimited amounts of coal, fossil fuels, and other minerals without any consequences. However, after about 300 years of industrial revolution and the intense production and consumption patterns being replicated all over the earth, it has become clear that we do not have infinite resources!

Question: How did this realization come about?

Answer: This realization is based on scientific data. You can look at it.

There was a study done by MIT researchers in 1972 called "Limits to Growth"[2] that outlined the fact that we are living on a planet with finite resources and unlimited growth in consumption of such resources is impossible to sustain forever.

2# https://en.wikipedia.org/wiki/The_Limits_to_Growth#:~:text=The%20Limits%20to%20
Growth%20(LTG,the%20Earth%20and%20human%20systems.

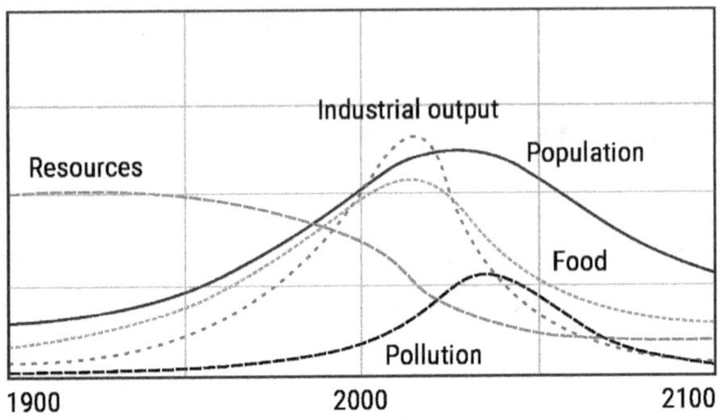

- BAU Computer Model for "World 3"
- Pollution and resource scarcity starts to impact
  ind.productn and then food in decades 2010-2030

From our own experience in these times, it has become clear that we do not have unlimited resources.

Take water for example. There is not enough fresh water on Earth to waste. We have only 3% fresh water on this planet and only 0.5% is actually in a usable form. Our indiscriminate use of fresh water has created a water shortage. By 2025, half of the world's population will live in water-stressed areas[3] . We lack free or low-cost land to continue building factories or extracting minerals, metals, coal or engaging in agriculture. Our forest cover is not endless, and we cannot continuously cut trees for wood-burning or other purposes. Additionally, we do not have an endless supply of fossil fuels to feed the ever-growing industrial and human consumption. All of this is well-documented in scientific studies.

3# https://www.pewtrusts.org/en/trend/archive/ spring-2019/a-map-of-the-future-of-water

Question: Yes, but we don't pay attention to these things.

Answer: The time has come to pay attention to these impacts human and industrial activity is having and has been having for quite some time. This is precisely why ESG is important.

Engine of growth for last 300 years: Rapid industrialization to pursue shareholder wealth maximization

Industrialization is the social and economic transformation of society from an agrarian to an industrial economy

PROBLEMS

Air and water pollution and soil contamination that resulted in a significant deterioration of quality of life and life expectancy.	Industrialization exacerbated the separation of labor and capital. Those who ouned the means of production became disproportionately rich, resulting in wider income inequality.	Workers were forced to leave their families and migrate to urban areas in search of jobs.	They worked long hours, were poorly nourished and lived in overcrowded conditions, which led to disease and stress.

Question: Ok, please tell me more.

Answer: Interestingly, our impact is not just one-sided; it's two-sided.

Question: What do you mean by that?

Answer: A company's relationship with natural resources has a two-sided impact. On one side, a company relies on these resources as inputs, leading to a unidirectional impact. If the resources are reducing, a company may not be able to manufacture its products or offer services. Depletion of resources can

significantly drive-up costs, as we are witnessing today. Access to essentials like water, fertile land, clean air is no longer free. We are paying for clean drinking water. We are paying to make land fertile, and we are buying and using air purifiers in large cities. Not only that, but the prices of these limited resources are also increasing steadily.

Fluctuations caused by sudden events like droughts, floods, hurricanes, storms, tsunamis, or man-made crises can also affect the availability of these resources. This can negatively impact companies and affect a larger segment of human population. For example, recent floods in Asia led to increased prices of various food items. Similarly, the Russia-Ukraine war increased the prices of wheat and other commodities.

Hence, understanding the risks that a company may have due to its dependence on natural resources is important to know, so the company can prepare for them and manage these risks. It directly affects its operations. These risks could be from either natural factors or a result of our deficiency.

In the context of ESG, this concept is known as 'single materiality,' where 'Single' stands for one-way impact, and 'Materiality' stands for significant or financially important impact. As we know, not all impacts are the same.

Question: So, what is double materiality then?

Answer: Well, a company not only consumes resources from the environment, but it also creates an output. So, when this output is put back into the environment, it then impacts the environment itself, that is double materiality.

Question: Please explain in more detail.

Answer: To elaborate further, consider that a company's outputs encompass more than just its products or services. For example, it creates waste materials. It is not going to use them and these need to be discarded. So, where will they go? What happens to these waste materials? The company will either burn them or dump them in a landfill? Perhaps with or without any treatment? If they choose to burn, it results in air pollution. On the other hand, if they go for landfilling, it leads to land pollution, right?

Question: Yes.

Answer: Similarly, a company releases many outputs into the environment such as wastewater from its factories, air pollutants, solid waste, carbon emissions, and other greenhouse gases, that are responsible for causing human induced climate change, plastics in food chain[4], and more.

4# https://www.plasticsoupfoundation.org/en/plastic-problem/

Question: Understood?

Answer: So, all these outputs that the company is putting back into the environment affect the environment. Typically, they pollute the natural surroundings. If only a handful of companies did this at a small scale, it would not have been a problem, similar to the situation during the late-18th century when the industrial revolution started.

However, given the current scenario of widespread and intense resource consumption worldwide fueled by globalization, the cumulative effects of all these human and industrial activities are resulting in a tremendous amount of pollution in the natural ecosystem. This pollution not only harms natural resources, diminishing Nature's budget of such resources, but also leads to the destruction of various other species. These effects might stem from routine business operations or from mismanagement. One example of mismanagement is the BP oil spill that happened in 2010.

Case Study: BP

In 2010, BP was the largest oil and gas company in the world, with operations in over 80 countries.

In April 2010, BP's Deepwater Horizon oil rig exploded in the Gulf of Mexico, causing the largest oil spill in US history.

The disaster caused severe environmental damage, with an estimated 4.9 million barrels of oil spilled into the Gulf of Mexico and resulting in significant economic losses for the region.

The disaster caused extensive environmental damage, including the death of wildlife, contamination of beaches and coastal wetlands, and damage to the fishing and tourism industries in the region. The regional economic impact of the disaster was estimated to be $8 Billion.

The disaster had a significant financial impact on BP. The company reported a loss of $40.9 Billion for the year, the largest loss in its history. At the height of the crisis, BP's share price had fallen by 50%, leading to a loss of $105 Billion worth of market value for its shareholders.

Overall, as of 2018, penalties, charges and clean-up costs had resulted in BP spending at least $65 Billion, and the company's reputation suffered significantly.

The disaster highlighted BP's failure to recognize and address the potential risks posed by its operations. BP had not adequately assessed the risks of an oil spill in the Gulf of Mexico and had failed to implement appropriate safety measures.

The drilling platform had been operating without a majority of the engineer-approved documents it needed to run safely, leaving the platform vulnerable to operator errors. BP failed to implement appropriate safety measures, such as rigorous maintenance and testing protocols, to ensure the integrity of the Deepwater Horizon oil rig.

Additionally, BP was unprepared for the disaster and had not taken the necessary steps to mitigate the potential consequences.

In July 2016, BP was ordered to pay a historic fine of $20.8 Billion[5], which is the highest corporate fine in history.

Question: So, was this a result of mismanagement? What impact do Business-as-usual operations have on the Natural Environment, and how does it affect us?

Answer: Yes, this incident happened because things were not managed well. We need to be conscious of the impact our business is having on the environment. Nature is a big interconnected system where everything affects everything else. What we do to nature comes back to us. For example, if we pollute the air, it doesn't just hurt people, but also plants and animals. A clear example is that there are fewer birds now compared to before. Anywhere between 3-4 Billion birds have been lost in the last 50 years. Around half of the world's bird species are in decline and 12% of the bird species are threatened with extinction[6].

If we continue our heavy dependence on burning of fossil fuels, we are also causing an increase in local and global average temperatures, which is called human-induced global warming, a major factor in climate change[7]. Have we not noticed that weather patterns are not the same as before?

5# https://www.nytimes.com/2015/10/06/business/bp-settlement-in-gulf-oil-spill-is-raised-to-20-8-Billion.html?mwgrp=c-dbar&smid=url-share

6# https://www.birdlife.org/papers-reports/state-of-the-worlds-birds-2022/

7# https://www.un.org/en/climatechange/science/causes-effects-climate-change

The unpredictable weather is bringing along extreme weather events like record-breaking heat waves, tsunamis, hurricanes, floods, droughts, earthquakes, landslides etc. These are causing significant damage to both life and economic activity. It is expected to wipe off 18% of Global GDP if left unchecked by 2050[8].

As a result of continuous increases in human and industrial activities, many species have been lost already. We have killed them, not even realizing that this is what we have done. Just take a look at the data on the loss of biodiversity. The Living Planet Report by WWF highlights that we have lost an average of 69% of species since 1970[9].

As if our impact on the land mass of Earth was not enough, we have also left our marks on the oceans. Oceans have become the biggest garbage dumping grounds of our lifestyle and industrial activity. We have been dumping plastic that chokes and kills marine life such as fish, tortoise, dolphins, sharks, and even whales! The sheer amount of plastic in the oceans is now visible from satellites[10]. In 1950 we were producing 2 milliontons of plastics. Now we are producing 450 million tons. But why do we have to dump it in the oceans? Why are we not handling it responsibly?

8# https://www.weforum.org/agenda/2021/06/impact-climate-change-global-gdp//

9# https://livingplanet.panda.org/en-IN/

10# Hannah Ritchie, Veronika Samborska and Max Roser (2023) - "Plastic Pollution" Published online at OurWorldInData.org. Retrieved from: 'https://ourworldindata.org/plastic-pollution' [Online Resource]

Besides, the satellites themselves, that have become a symbol of human progress, also leave their debris at the end of their lifecycle. This debris remains in orbit just above the earth's atmosphere, making future space travel extremely risky for us[11].

So, we have left no corner untouched. We have polluted the land, the oceans, the air and even space!

Question: Wow! I had no idea that our impact on the natural environment was this significant!

Answer: Yes, this is the core of the issue. We are used to thinking about things that impact our limited personal space - our home or office. We do not think of the cumulative impact at the level of the planet Earth. We lack a holistic perspective and fail to consider how our actions affect others. We only think about ourselves.

Question: However, in the long run, it will affect our life also, won't it?

Answer: Absolutely, this is already happening. We cannot ignore the consequences of our actions. The effects are not something for the distant future; they are unfolding quickly.

11# https://www.britannica.com/technology/space-debris

The earth's ecosystem has become fragile, unable to cope with even small changes without tipping the balance. As a result, we are witnessing an increasing amount and severity of natural catastrophes. For example, consider the floods that hit Bengaluru, India, in September 2022, which flooded 7700 homes and caused a direct financial loss of INR 340 Crores (USD 41 Million).

On the other hand, the floods in Pakistan in 2022 caused a loss of 1700 lives, damaged or destroyed more than 2.2 million houses, affected 33 million people, and submerged one third of the country. The economic losses were estimated at around USD 30 Billion.

We need to urgently learn to live in balance and harmony with nature, to remember that we are a part of nature, and nature is a part of us. If we don't pay attention to what we are adding to nature, nature will bring it back to us, and that will be the only way for us to realize. There is no other way as nature always works in cycles. What we give to it is what we will get back. So, it is better to remain careful and pay attention.

Sustainability, in simple terms, is all about maintaining balance and taking responsibility for our actions and their consequences.

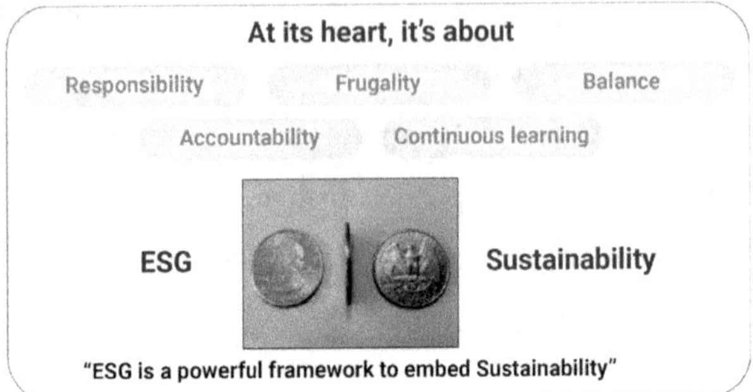

ESG is simply one type of a framework to achieve Sustainability.

Question: How is it about being Responsible and Accountable? What can companies do about it?

Answer: In Economics, there is this concept of 'externality'. It is defined as an indirect cost or benefit to an uninvolved third party that arises as an effect of another party's activity. It means that our actions will have a cascading effect on someone else. It simply means the impact we are having on others, without their permission or knowledge. More specifically, we're referring to the negative impacts here.

For example, consider driving a regular car. The exhaust gases that are produced on burning the fuel are an example of externality. We are not directly paying for causing that pollution. So, who bears the cost? Apparently, it might seem like no one in financial terms. However, over a period of time, the costs become apparent. Where? In the form of respiratory diseases that are caused to people in a city and the medical expenses they have to bear. It also costs the governments to provide health care or subsidize it. In densely populated cities like Delhi, people are also forced to buy air purifiers to be able to breathe less polluted air. All these expenses stem from externalities like air pollution that were never considered before. But now, these costs are evident and on a significant scale.

Now, if a manufacturing company does not take into account the air pollution it is producing, then the air pollution remains as an 'externality'. Even though the company causes it, the impact is felt by everyone. This has been a challenge with the traditional economic growth model over the past 300 years. Many outputs of a business and human activities were left as 'externalities' that the activity did not take into account on its own. Whether it's wastewater, air pollution, or plastic waste that goes into landfill, these were often not considered. When a few entities did this, the impact on the natural ecosystem was minor. However, given the global scope of human and economic activities, with numerous business organizations following this pattern on a large scale all over the world, the consequences are now becoming evident in nature and life.

Climate change caused by excess production of Greenhouse gas emissions – is an example of externality. Air pollution fits the same category. The pollution of land and oceans with plastics is another example.

When the actual economic cost of inputs and outputs from any business activity are not measured, not paid, or accounted for by that business's calculations, externalities emerge. These are costs that someone else or the entire society has to pay. This is why there have been efforts to assign a price to carbon emissions – to make companies that are producing more carbon to pay for it.

Hence, being responsible and accountable means taking into account the impact or the externalities we are causing, especially the negative ones.

If we look at the business transactions, most companies are part of a chain of activities either as suppliers or customers of other companies that are inter-dependent on each other. This structure is called the supply chain or, more accurately, the value chain.

The entire value chain needs to become responsible and accountable and reduce its impact or externalities, especially the negative ones.

This, in economic terms, is known as 'internalizing' the cost of externalities. Essentially, a responsible company would incorporate the cost of its impact into its financial calculations, and it would openly disclose and report the 'true economic cost' of its operations.

Question: Okay, I understand now.

Answer: That's great. Returning to the concept of double materiality, it implies paying attention to the two-way interactions: the impact the natural environment has on the company (and its financial performance) as well as the impact the company has on the natural environment. This second form of materiality can also be measured in financial terms. A company can either reduce the environmental assets or increase them. In the former, it has a negative impact on the environment, in the latter, a positive impact.

Question: I see, thanks.

Answer: Most ESG assessment frameworks, including sophisticated ESG rating models, typically consider only single materiality, which involves a one-way impact. For example, the financial impact of the environment on a company. Meaning, how the environment is affecting the company and how the company is managing those resources or risks coming from its dependence on those resources.

Double materiality is a relatively new concept, and it is yet to find application in the most commonly used ESG frameworks or rating models. However, I am mentioning it here so that you can use it as a central part of your ESG thinking whenever you apply it to any problem or situation.

Question: There is a lot of concern these days about Climate Change. What can a company do about this?

Answer: The Climate sub-theme within the Environment pillar focuses on managing a company's climate-related risks and opportunities. Excessive human-generated greenhouse gas emissions are the primary driver of climate change. These gases trap heat in the atmosphere, some occurring naturally and being emitted through natural processes, while others are created and emitted solely through human activities. The primary greenhouse gases produced due to human activities are carbon dioxide, methane, nitrous oxide, hydrofluorocarbons, perfluorocarbons, and sulfur hexafluoride.

Many human and business activities rely heavily on coal and fossil fuels, which release greenhouse gases. Greater economic activity results in more fossil fuel consumption. Fossil fuels – coal, oil and gas – are the largest contributor to global climate change, accounting for over 75 per cent of global greenhouse gas emissions and nearly 90 per cent of all carbon dioxide emissions[12]. Companies need to measure their GHG emissions, report them, and eventually find ways to reduce these emissions. This applies both to their internal operations and their broader value chain.

12# https://www.un.org/en/climatechange/science/causes-effects-climate-change#:~:text=Fossil%20 fuels%20%E2%80%93%20coal%2C%20oil%20and,of%20all%20carbon%20dioxide%20emissions.

Question: What does Net Zero mean?

Answer: Net Zero means that the amount of greenhouse gas emissions that are being produced is equal to the amount being absorbed. It means that the 'net' impact on the environment in terms of greenhouse gas emissions is zero.

This can be measured at different levels, such as individual processes, products or services, companies, or even countries. If a company does not produce any net greenhouse gas emissions, then it is implied that it has reached 'Net Zero'. The company can achieve this result by either stopping to produce any greenhouse gas emissions from its activities (for example, by using renewable energy and clean technologies or decarbonization of its activities) or by deciding to absorb any greenhouse gases it produces, for example by purchasing carbon credits or planting trees, sufficient enough to offset its own greenhouse gas emissions. Of course, rigor, transparency and verification are essential ingredients to establish trustin these efforts.

Question: So, what actions should companies take to ensure their environmental performance in the long run?

Answer: Long-term environmental sustainability is a crucial aspect of a company's performance that focuses on the natural resources used, their efficiency, and the waste produced.

It includes a range of sub-themes such as pollution, material usage, energy efficiency, water usage, carbon emissions, and the

overall performance of products throughout their life cycle. In recent years, there has been a growing consensus that businesses need to adopt a "regenerative" approach, working to restore the natural ecosystem as an integral part of their business activities.

Following the industrial revolution, economic activities have increased manifold, leading to the realization that there are limits to the natural resources that can be consumed. Additionally, the waste produced poses a threat to humanity, biodiversity, and the overall natural ecosystem. We are dealing with challenges that include air pollution, water pollution, land pollution, greenhouse gas emissions, and toxic waste. The impacts of these pollutants include the discovery of poisonous chemicals and microplastics in food, soil infertility, and ocean biosphere destruction.

As a result, companies are now expected to be carbon-neutral, net-zero greenhouse gas emitters, and water-neutral, in the minimum, among other objectives. Such efforts benefit both the environment and the company's bottom line, as resource-efficient practices reduce costs and improve profit margins. For example, mining companies have realized that in some cases, it is cheaper to recycle minerals instead of mining them from the ground.

However, the natural ecosystem has been destroyed to such an extent that being resource-efficient is no longer sufficient. There is now an emerging consensus that businesses must be

"regenerative" in nature. This means they must restore the natural ecosystem as an integral part of their business activities, such as creating carbon sinks, recharging the water table, regenerating the land, increasing forest cover, establishing bio-reserves to rehabilitate species, and cleaning up the oceans.

Companies should actively seek opportunities to improve their performance by:

1. Tapping into energy efficiency improvements and replacing traditional energy sources or technologies with new, renewable options can be achieved through:

   Biofuels like biodiesel, biogas, ethanol, etc.

   Renewable sources of energy like solar, wind, tidal, etc.

   Alternative sources of energy like hydrogen, fuel cells, etc.

   Adoption of electric cars or hybrid.

   Implementation of green building practices.

   Exploring other cleantech opportunities.

2. Improving material usage efficiency, with the long-term goal of achieving 100% recycling.

3. Beginning with waste minimization and recycling initiatives, with the eventual aim of achieving zero waste operations over time.

4. Seeking to increase the use of sustainable materials with the least impact on the natural environment.

5. Striving for circularity in material use, where all materials used in an operation are recycled, removing the need to extract new materials from the Earth. This approach contributes to a circular economy.

6. Work towards reducing the use of natural resources, ultimately aiming for net positive outcomes. Net positive operations involve putting back more resources into the environment than those that were consumed.

7. Developing new products, services, technologies, and business models that are part of a solution instead of being part of the problem.

Being part of the solution means that these products, services, technologies, and business models have a positive impact on the natural environment. Thus, they reverse the damage caused till date and regenerate the natural environment. In doing so, they not only create revenue opportunities for the business but also contribute to the restoration of natural capital.

There are many examples of such solutions that are regenerative. For example:

- Carbon sequestration technologies: Products and solutions that extract carbon emissions from the environment and store them, helping them to combat climate change. Textile products made from Hemp is an example.

- Eco-Friendly Factories: Factories that create a positive environmental influence by providing clean air and water to the natural environment instead of depleting these resources.

- Sustainable Agriculture Systems: Farming methods that not only foster healthier and hygienic food production but also regenerate soil and ecosystems.

However, working on these solutions requires commitment, an open mindset, creativity, and perseverance to develop, test, and scale them.

Question: Thank you, this has been very helpful! Now, we've discussed the Environment pillar of ESG. Could you also explain the other two pillars - S and G?

Answer: Why Not? Just turn this page and you will get your answers!!!

"The world has enough for everyone's need, but not enough for everyone's greed."
                                      - Mahatma Gandhi

Chapter 2

What is S?

Let us now understand the S pillar.

The Social aspect of a company's activities falls under the S pillar. What could they be? It includes all the interactions the company has with various social entities. This involves the employees working within the company, all the customers that the company is serving, all those potential customers that it could reach but isn't doing so currently, all the suppliers that it is taking inputs from, and the connections with communities where it has operations or those that are in the neighborhood. All these interactions with its stakeholders' form part of the S pillar.

Some examples: Whether the company provides equal opportunities for its employees, respects the freedom of association for its workforce, ensures the health and safety of workers and employees during operations, avoids any human rights violations, steers clear of child labor, and takes responsibility for the impact its products have on the lives of its customers, among other considerations.

Question: But how does this affect the company? Why is this important?

Answer: Just like a company uses resources from the natural environment and leaves its output back in the natural environment, in the same way, every company uses resources from its social environment. A company is not solely comprised of buildings, machines, factories, shops, IT servers, technology etc. It is full of social interactions. It is fundamentally about people.

These constant interactions, both within and outside the company, can be categorized into two types: if these interactions with the company create win-win value for the interacting stakeholder and that value is shared fairly between the company and the concerned stakeholder, then the company is doing an excellent job of managing its Social (S) pillar and will remain successful for a long time to come.

On the other hand, if the company interacts with its employees, for example, and fails to give them good working conditions, neglects their well-being, or worse, offers lower compensation than the market standard, how long do you think these employees will remain loyal to that company?

Question: I see the point.

Answer: So, this will have a direct financial impact on the company. If more and more employees leave the company, it will have to hire new ones to replace them. Think about the

expenses associated with hiring new employees and providing them with training. Calculate the loss caused when the most experienced employees leave. How much value gets lost! That is the intellectual capital of the company. It loses an asset, called Human Capital, and this can be quantified, even though it is difficult to quantify it precisely. It can be estimated approximately.

Question: That is a loss.

Answer: Now, imagine if the same company manages its employees well, takes care of them. If it ensures their well-being, offers competitive compensation or even better, motivates them to stay, empowers them to implement their ideas, allows them to experiment and learn from failures, fosters a culture that allows and encourages creativity, supports them in the difficult times of their life like sickness, maternity or paternity, and provides healthcare coverage, encourages them to pursue higher education, learning and development, upskilling, and even offers them an equitable share of its profits or equity in the firm - how do you think employees would respond? Will they not consider the company as their own? As their well-wisher? Will they not give their best to their work? Will they not create innovation, new ideas to save cost, improve profits, grow the business, serve more customers, and create superior products and services?

Most importantly, when these employees come in contact with the customers of the company, or in neighboring communities, what will these other stakeholders learn about the company? That it is a great organization to work at, one that genuinely cares for its people. Consider the impact: existing customers of such a company will likely remain loyal with the company and come back to do more business with such a company. How about the potential customers? Would they not be excited and inspired to work with such a company?

Question: Yes, that's a powerful effect.

Answer: If the employees of a company are its fans, then they naturally will become brand ambassadors of this company. In such a scenario, does the company really need to invest heavily in expensive advertisements to attract more employees or customers?

Question: Absolutely not!

Answer: Exactly. This is the premise of the S pillar and, in fact, the entire ESG framework. Companies that effectively manage all their capitals well, not just the financial capital, do well. This includes stakeholder capital, which forms the S pillar, as well as natural capital forming the E pillar and governance capital composing the G pillar.

Question: Does this cover everything about the S pillar?

Answer: Not quite. In a similar way, if the company takes care of its other social stakeholders like customers, potential customers, suppliers, and communities where it operates, it can gain from those interactions by creating win-win value and

sharing it fairly between itself and the respective stakeholders. The logic is that the company cannot grow forever by ignoring or harming its stakeholders.

If the company does not provide better value than its competitors, its customers will switch away from that company.

If the company does not provide better value to its potential customers, they will not have an incentive to become customers of this company.

If the suppliers do not flourish and prosper while working with the company, then how will the company manage its future supplies?

Question: However, many large companies overcome this challenge by keeping multiple suppliers and try not to depend on any one of them.

Answer: Yes, that's true. However, a different level of value emerges when the suppliers truly become a part of the company's future growth story. They may provide ideas for improvement, act as catalysts for future innovation, and strengthen the competitive advantage of the company.

In contrast, consider a scenario where suppliers work under constant fear of losing the relationship at any time, leading them to accept low margins and challenging payment terms.

Question: What is the problem with that? Is this not how the business world works?

Answer: In this approach, the relationship is transactional. It lacks a long-term relationship. As a result, it will most likely not create long term win-win for both. Instead, it could lead to incidents like the Rana Plaza tragedy in Bangladesh.

Case Study: 1100 workers died at Rana Plaza in Bangladesh

Garment suppliers, catering to some of the largest apparel brands in the world, were so squeezed under low margins and ever competitive prices over many years, that they did not have the resources to invest in improving the safety of their crumbling factories.

As a result, 1100 garment workers died when a building collapsed in Bangladesh in 2013[13]. All the top global fashion brands buy their garments from Bangladesh. Only after the Rana Plaza tragedy, the 2013 Accord on Fire and Building Safety – a legally binding contract to ensure garment workers in Bangladesh have a safe working environment – was signed by more than 200 brands globally, including the likes of H&M, Inditex (owner of Zara) and Adidas.

Question: Wow, I did not know about this.

13# thttps://en.wikipedia.org/wiki/Rana_Plaza_collapse

Answer: Absolutely, we usually see only positive stories about a company or industry. Negative stories usually remain hidden unless a significant crisis forces them into the spotlight. Now imagine the impact on branding of a company if an avoidable human tragedy like this happens.

Question: This was avoidable?

Answer: Of course! If the buyer brands would have paid sufficient margins to the supplier factories, if they would have noticed the crumbling state of the infrastructure during their supplier visits, this disaster could have been averted. Additionally, if government licensing officers had been attentive, then this tragedy would not have happened and 1100 people would have been saved.

This is not the only example of poor management of the social impact of a company. There are many others like this. The Bhopal Gas Tragedy was also really bad – it's one of the worst industrial disasters in history.

Case Study: Poisonous gas leak causing Bhopal Gas Tragedy

The Bhopal Gas Tragedy happened on December 2nd, 1984[14] when a gas leak occurred at a pesticide plant owned by Union Carbide India Limited (UCIL). This leak released toxic gas in

---

14# https://en.wikipedia.org/wiki/Bhopal_disaster

the atmosphere. The disaster resulted in the deaths of thousands of people and many more suffered from health problems that lasted a long time. The disaster was caused by a lack of safety measures at the UCIL pesticide plant and inadequate response to the emergency situation. Union Carbide faced significant backlash from stakeholders and the company's stock price dropped by 50% in the weeks following the disaster. In 1989, Union Carbide agreed to pay $470 million to the Indian government to settle the matter.

This tragic event shows how important it is for companies to be responsible and think about the well-being of people. The disaster had a devastating impact on the lives and livelihoods of the people of Bhopal. From a governance perspective, the tragedy raises questions about the responsibility of corporations for their actions and the need for greater accountability and transparency.

Case Study: Data abuse allegations at Cambridge Analytica and Facebook

The scandal involved the British political consulting firm, Cambridge Analytica, and its alleged improper use of Facebook data to influence political campaigns, that broke out in 2018[15]. This incident raised serious concerns about privacy violations and ethical practices. Cambridge Analytica reportedly accessed

---

15# https://en.wikipedia.org/wiki/Facebook%E2%80%93Cambridge_Analytica_data_scandal

data from millions of Facebook users without their consent and then used this data to develop targeted political ads and messages for the 2016 U.S. Presidential campaign. This manipulation of data sparked investigations in both the United States and the United Kingdom, accusing the firm of breaching users' privacy and manipulating public opinions.

Eventually, Cambridge Analytica declared bankruptcy in 2018 and was subsequently dissolved, while Facebook, too, faced strong public backlash and regulatory scrutiny. Following the scandal, Facebook's market value dropped by more than $50 Billion, and the company's shares experienced a sharp decline of more than 20%.

The scandal serves as a cautionary tale about the risks of data misuse, privacy violations, and also highlights the need for greater transparency, regulatory oversight and accountability from companies that collect personal data.

Companies that deal with data of their users, for example tech services and platforms, banks and financial services, health care providers, and digital public goods organizations, need to take due care in using, storing and handling data to maintain the trust of their users.

Case Study: Safety of Maggi Noodles (Nestle)

Back in 2015, the Indian government took action by recalling Maggi noodles due to concerning test results that uncovered the presence of high levels of lead and monosodium glutamate (MSG) in the product[16]. The company was forced to recall products worth millions, and the Maggi brand was even banned in several states in India.

Following this recall, Nestle, the company behind Maggi noodles, reported a loss of over USD 70 million in the second quarter of 2015. The company's share price also dropped significantly in the aftermath of the scandal, and it took several months for the company to regain its footing in the Indian market.

In response to the crisis, Nestle implemented a number of ESG-related initiatives like increased testing of products, improved supply chain management, and more transparent communication with their stakeholders

This underscores the importance of product safety for its consumers, which is an important aspect of the social performance of the company. Ensuring the safety of products is an essential part of maintaining the trust of consumers.

Case Study: Child labor in Nestle's cocoa supply chain

In 2005, Nestle faced severe backlash in the case involving allegations of child labor in the company's cocoa supply chain

---

16# https://en.wikipedia.org/wiki/Maggi_noodles_safety_concerns_in_India

in the Ivory Coast[17], including the use of child labor, forced labor, and unsafe working conditions. It was revealed that Nestle had not implemented adequate policies and procedures to prevent these serious issues.

The publicity and reputational damage caused by the labor-related issues had a significant impact on the company's brand and image. The company also faced pressure from investors and ESG advocates.

One of the biggest outcomes of this case was the establishment of the company's Child Labor Monitoring and Remediation System (CLMRS), a comprehensive program designed to identify and address child labor risks in Nestle's cocoa supply chain. In 2019, Nestle reported that it had identified and remediated 18,283 cases of child labor in its cocoa supply chain in the Ivory Coast and Ghana. The company also reported helping more than 78,000 children through its child labor awareness and education programs to combat child labor.

Question: So, there are real consequences?

Answer: Yes, there are indeed real and serious consequences if we do not pay attention to ESG. In its earlier years, most people used to dismiss ESG as something only philosophical, meant for environmentalists, TreeHuggers, social activists, or those considered 'woke,' etc. Some people continue with this criticism.

17#Schrage, Elliot J., and Anthony P. Ewing. "The cocoa industry and child labour *." The Journal of Corporate Citizenship, no. 18, summer 2005, pp. 99+. Gale Academic OneFile, link.gale.com/apps/doc/A135662776/AONE?u=anon~28356c1d&sid=googleScholar&xid=d90c5511. Accessed 1 Jan. 2024.

However, there is sufficient evidence now that ESG makes DIRECT BUSINESS SENSE. As a result, there is a greater consensus among all types of stakeholders about the need to apply ESG principles. Just consider this: several surveys[18] conducted among retail consumers in multiple markets have shown that people are willing to pay a premium for products that are positive in their ESG impact[19]. They also show a willingness to invest in funds and companies with higher ESG ratings[20]. Therefore, a company's long-term prosperity relies on paying attention to ESG aspects. It's crucial to consistently monitor, measure and track its performance based on ESG parameters. It is also in the self-interest of the company to have a positive ESG strategy for the long term.

This is the interesting part of ESG principles – if we do well at the core of the business and focus there, we will also make profits in the end. Profits will come naturally. However, if we keep the focus on profits and only profits and neglect other aspects, we risk losing the overall game in the long run.

Unfortunately, companies do not realize that in the pursuit of short-term profits, they may compromise the very core of their business. For example, letting go of employees to boost quarterly or yearly profits might seem profitable at first, but what

---

18# https://globescan.com/trends/healthy-sustainable-living/

19# https://www.kantar.com/campaigns/who-cares-who-does-in-the-fmcg-industry

20# https://www.cfainstitute.org/-/media/documents/survey/future-of-sustainability.ashx

about the loss of talent, experience, and the intellectual property that these employees brought to the table?

Question: Is all firing bad then?

Answer: Well, it should be the last resort. If a business is shutting down, then there is no choice. Similarly, if a business is changing its business model and will not need certain roles in the future, then there is logic. However, even in such cases, it is worth trying if the employees can be re-trained and deployed somewhere else. If we can't do any of that, then the company can certainly try to place them somewhere else, in another job, in another organization or help them pursue other livelihood options, after getting them the right training. If we abruptly fire people and take away their livelihood suddenly, then the company is causing a negative impact, and this will come back to the company one day.

Question: So, what about the sudden firings happening worldwide?

Answer: Certainly, it shows the principles of the companies who are firing their key assets: their employees. It shows that such companies clearly value profits more than people. Hence all their talk about ESG or Sustainability is a myth. Such companies are simply greenwashing.

Question: What is greenwashing?

Answer: Greenwashing is when a company tries to exaggerate or mis-represent its performance on Sustainability or ESG. When you say you are a Sustainable company in your reports, but you don't actually implement it where it matters. This is simply misleading the investors and the other stakeholders.

Question: Why do companies engage in greenwashing?

Answer: As they want to show that they are responsible companies and good brands by signing up to ESG and Sustainability frameworks, standards etc. They want to enjoy the benefits of being perceived as an ESG compliant company potentially to boost their brand and market price. However, the reality is quite different. At their core, they are doing business as usual.

Question: So, there are intentional green washers in the market?

Answer: Yes, there are a lot of companies out there who greenwash. Greenwashing is of two types: Conscious and Unconscious. Unconscious is when companies greenwash without even realizing it. They may not understand how to apply the specific ESG principles.

However, Conscious greenwashing is where a company knowingly misrepresents its performance or initiatives on ESG.

These companies are keen to reap the rewards of ESG and Sustainability without doing the hard work it takes to become one. It's important to be realistic about this aspect when you take up a job or build your career in such a company.

Question: Why?

Answer: Because the green washers will never gain the true and full benefits of implementing ESG in their business. They may gain attention in the short term, but in the long run, they will lose out to their competitors.

Question: Do you have data to support this?

Answer: There is indeed data to consider. If you look at the average lifespan of the Fortune 500 companies[21], you might notice something interesting: every 13 years, half of the companies in that list disappear.[22]

Question: Why?

Answer: They become irrelevant. They lose touch with their customers, especially those who are potential customers. As a result, their business is no longer valuable. Remember Nokia? They were the market leader for many years in the mobile phone market. Remember Kodak? They were the king of the camera market.

21# https://www.kauffman.org/wp-content/uploads/2012/06/fortune_500_turnover.pdf

22# https://ryanberman.com/glossary/business-apocalypse/#

When a company stops creating value for both their customers and non-customers, when it does not pay attention to its stakeholders then this is the result, in the long run. While these changes might not become apparent from one quarter to next, or even from one financial year to another, they do manifest over time. Patience is required to observe these outcomes.

Question: How can we predict, ahead of time, which company will end up going this way?

Answer: When a company gets so obsessed with its financial results and share price that it stops looking at its stakeholders then this is bound to happen. This happens when they stop asking these questions:

"Am I creating value for my stakeholders? How much?

Is their quality of life getting better because of my business?"

When executives spend more time in their offices and less time engaging with their customers, and do not experience what their customers and suppliers are experiencing, then this outcome is inevitable.

ESG, as a framework, delivers long term value for a company - provided that the company genuinely embraces ESG principles and avoids any form of greenwashing.

Question: Sure, but how can one know which company is greenwashing and which one is not? Especially for someone like me who is just starting out my ESG journey?

Answer: This is very simple! Just examine their reports, public statements, announcements etc. Watch what they say and compare it to what they actually do – especially their day-to-day decisions and actions, particularly during difficult times. Then you will be able to see if there is any gap between their public position and their actions. If there is a gap, they are likely engaging in greenwashing. If there is no gap, then you have someone following ESG genuinely.

Question: Wonderful, this is a good key.

Answer: Yes, and when you find a company, group or team that genuinely practices ESG and lives up to their commitments, it's wise to engage with them and collaborate with them. These entities are the future leaders of tomorrow. Such companies, groups, or teams consistently generate value that surpasses expectations, ensuring their sustained success. That is going to be a winning team!

Question: But wait a minute, what about companies that have large gaps in their ESG policy versus their practice? Should we avoid working with them altogether?

Answer: Not necessary. We need to be realistic and practical, without being judgmental. If we notice that a company has a gap between their policy and practice but is genuinely motivated to bridge that gap, then it is perfectly fine to work with them and help them reduce that gap.

Question: But how can one know if they are really keen to remove that gap?

Answer: They must have a clear intention, which they are able to demonstrate, with clear tangible commitments that they have already made or are about to make. In such cases, it is worth working with such a company and helping them begin their ESG journey or accelerate it.

Question: What are the other benefits for the company by starting to focus on the S pillar?

Answer: A company might currently be serving only a part of the society. For example, pharmaceutical companies that develop new drugs to address highly profitable lifestyle diseases but ignore drug research for diseases affecting the poor. This has led to initiatives like the campaign for "Access to Essential Medicines" asking drug companies to develop medicines for diseases like malaria and tuberculosis, which impact a much larger section of the society. Historically, research on these diseases has received lesser than 1% of research and development (R&D) spending from major pharmaceutical companies[23].

Society has several needs that are being fulfilled currently by companies that serve them and many other needs that are yet to be fulfilled.

23# https://www.ncbi.nlm.nih.gov/pmc/articles/PMC1200561/

Within these unmet needs lies an opportunity for companies to make a difference. This opportunity can be divided into two parts. First, addressing needs that currently exist in society but have not been fulfilled. Example, developing drugs for diseases affecting the poor. Second, identifying needs that have not been recognized or explicitly understood, such as innovations in healthcare systems that could eliminate the need for certain drugs altogether.

A company that can identify and fulfill unmet needs has the opportunity to create value for the society. As a result, it receives a share of this value from the society in terms of increased demand for its existing products and services or the demand for new products or services.

Any company has the ability to contribute, via its activities, to the growth and sustainability of the economy and society in which it operates. This is possible when the company pays attention to the unmet needs of the society. Questions like these become crucial:

- Who are the untapped potential customers?

- Why are we not serving them currently?

- Do we have existing products and services to cater to them?

- If not, can we create new products and services to cater to those unmet needs?

Extensive research has shown that targeting a broader section of the society often referred to as the 'Base of the Pyramid[24], segment gives companies access to new markets and revenue opportunities.

Question: That is great! So, what else should we know about the basics of ESG, to begin our journey?

Answer: Now, let us understand more about 'G'. So, why wait? Turn one more page!!!

24# term coined by Prof. Stuart Hart, along with C K Prahalad: https://www.strategy-business.com/article/11518

Chapter 3

What is G?

We need to understand the 'G' in ESG. It stands for Governance or Corporate Governance.

Corporate Governance is about how the company governs itself. How does it run? How is its Board like? - the topmost supervisory body in the company. What is the Board composition, and what are their roles and responsibilities? Whether the right capabilities exist in the Board or not?

The same principle applies to the company's top leadership. Are they effective? How are they incentivized? What is the relationship between the Board and the top management? What are the differences in pay between leadership and the average employee? What are the company's policies related to gender and other diversity parameters? What about policies related to bribery, corruption, business ethics? How well does the company and its leadership comply with regulations? What are the rights of shareholders, among many more parameters?

Question: Why is all this relevant?

Answer: Well, the larger the company, the more complex its organizational structure becomes. Therefore, there is a need to efficiently and effectively manage the functioning of a complex organization; otherwise, it will not produce the results we expect. Additionally, regulations exist that demand that public listed companies need to follow an approved governance code of conduct and policy framework. Hence, there is a legal requirement for large companies to follow a mandated governance structure and set of policies.

In addition, there are expectations from investors for it to follow 'good governance' practices.

Question: I understand the regulatory part, but why do we need to follow 'good governance' practices?

Answer: The investment capital of a large number of small investors is at stake: all the people who invest their savings in the stock market. The company cannot play with them. It must implement necessary good governance practices to safeguard the interest of these small investors who have invested their life's savings in the shares of that company. There have been many cases where investors lost their capital due to a lack of good governance.

Question: Do these governance requirements really make a difference?

Answer: Well, the answer is both yes and no. They are designed to provide a structure that can help. However, even with such a structure in place, there's always a chance that someone could exploit it to harm the interests of small investors. Every now and then we see cases like Enron[25] or Satyam where deliberate fraud has been committed by the management or leadership of some companies.

However, this again illustrates the point that ESG as a framework can actually help investors and companies if we use it properly.

Question: How?

Answer: Well, if we use the parameters in a company's G pillar, then we can distinguish, ahead of time, whether that company is handling its Governance well or not. This allows us to assess whether it is generating value through its corporate governance or destroying it.

Question: Can you explain in more detail please?

Answer: Just like a national or federal government of a country sets up its rules, regulations, policing mechanisms, and provides an array of government officers and hierarchy to govern

---

25# https://www.investopedia.com/updates/enron-scandal-summary/

the country, in a similar way, Corporate Governance of a company implies setting up the company policies, setting up roles and responsibilities to administer those policies, and govern the people involved. It includes mechanisms to ensure everything will work appropriately.

Therefore, Corporate Governance, from an ESG point of view can be reduced to two dimensions: Structure and Behavior. When a company establishes the correct structure and enables the right behavior among its management and employees, it can never go wrong.

Question: What constitutes the structure?

Answer: It consists of internal policies, processes, review mechanisms, and roles. What kind of relationships exist between these elements? Obviously, the entire structure has to be fit to deliver the purpose of the company. Only then it can create value.

Question: Great, so what is included in behavior?

Answer: When a company implements the right incentives, it systematically encourages certain types of desirable behaviors within the organization and discourages everything else.

For example, in a manufacturing type of company, health and safety is a very important factor. To encourage labor and management to innovate and co-create better health and safety practices, the company can set policies that provide for training

programs, set budgets for them, and encourage open communication. Both management and labor can then demonstrate discipline in following these policies. As a fool proof mechanism, it can also have a whistleblowing policy and system that helps labor report anything that goes against the company's stated policies, without fear of persecution.

The level of corporate behavior that a company achieves is the litmus test of its maturity.

Question: How can we know the maturity of a company?

Answer: We can assess its maturity by checking if it has any conflicts with any of its stakeholders.

Companies that are seasoned and mature demonstrate a consistent and reliable corporate behavior that is free from conflicts with either its internal or external stakeholders.

Mature companies have 100% alignment between their Corporate Governance aspirations and corporate behavior.

Companies that are facing conflicts with internal or external stakeholders are likely experiencing these issues due to discrepancies between their corporate behavior and their Corporate Governance aspirations.

Here, we present several case studies that we can examine in relation to this topic.

Case study: Wells Fargo

One well-known case from the services sector that demonstrates the gap between aspirations and behavior, resulting in a heavy loss, is the scandal involving Wells Fargo, a US-based financial services company[26].

In 2016, it was revealed that Wells Fargo had opened millions of unauthorized accounts in the names of their customers, without their knowledge or consent. These unauthorized accounts included credit card accounts, checking accounts, savings accounts, and more.

The practice began in 2011 and continued until 2016, when it was uncovered by regulators like the Consumer Financial Protection Bureau (CFPB). The company also faced investigations from other agencies, including the Securities and Exchange Commission (SEC) and the Department of Justice (DOJ) in the US.

The unethical behavior was driven by aggressive sales targets and incentive programs that rewarded employees for meeting these targets. Employees who met their quotas received bonuses and promotions, while those who did not were subject to disciplinary action, including termination. This environment fostered a culture of pressure and fear that encouraged employees to engage in fraudulent practices.

26# https://en.wikipedia.org/wiki/Wells_Fargo_cross-selling_scandal

The Wells Fargo scandal had significant consequences for the company, its employees, customers, and stakeholders. Some of them included:

- Financial losses: Wells Fargo paid over $3 Billion in fines and settlements related to the scandal, and its stock price declined by more than 25%.

- Reputational damage: The scandal damaged the company's reputation, resulting in a loss of customer trust, negative media coverage, and a decline in employee morale.

- Legal challenges: Wells Fargo faced a wave of customer lawsuits related to the unauthorized accounts, resulting in additional financial costs and reputational damage.

- Changes in leadership and governance: The scandal resulted in the resignation of the company's CEO and the appointment of a new leadership team, as well as changes in the company's governance practices.

The Wells Fargo scandal provides several lessons for companies in the services sector and beyond, including:

- The importance of ESG principles: Companies must prioritize ESG principles, including ethical behavior, risk management, and governance. By doing so, they can secure long-term sustainability and shield themselves from potential reputational and financial risks.

- The role of corporate culture: Companies must promote a culture of accountability, transparency, and ethical behavior in order to prevent fraudulent practices and other unethical behaviors.

- The importance of effective governance: Companies must have effective governance practices, including oversight and accountability from the board of directors and senior executives. Such measures are crucial for ensuring compliance with regulations and ethical standards.

- The need for effective risk management: Companies must have effective risk management practices in place to identify and address potential risks before they escalate into significant problems.

- The importance of customer trust: Companies must prioritize building and maintaining customer trust in order to ensure long-term success and sustainability.

If Wells Fargo had respected ESG principles, it could have avoided the significant losses and consequences that resulted from the unauthorized account scandal.

In response to the scandal, Wells Fargo implemented a number of changes to its business practices and corporate culture. These measures included the elimination of sales quotas, the introduction of a new code of ethics, and the creation of a new

risk management framework. The company also appointed a new CEO, Charlie Scharf, in 2019, who made rebuilding trust with customers and regulators a top priority.

Case Study: Satyam

The Satyam scandal was a corporate fraud case that occurred in India in 2009[27]. The company's founder and chairman, Ramalinga Raju, confessed to manipulating the company's accounts and inflating profits to the tune of over $1 Billion. The scandal resulted in the company's collapse, with many of its employees losing their jobs, and investors losing significant amounts of money.

The company suffered a loss of market value of around $2 Billion, in addition to damages to their reputation. To mitigate the issue, the new board of directors took steps to stabilize the company's operations and finances. The Indian government also introduced new regulations and governance frameworks to ensure greater transparency, governance and accountability in the corporate sector.

The scandal served as a powerful reminder of the imperative for effective regulation and oversight to prevent such fraudulent activities and to ensure that companies operate in a responsible and sustainable manner.

27# https://en.wikipedia.org/wiki/Satyam_scandal

Case Study: BYJU'S

Byju's, India's leading high growth edtech platform, established in 2011, recently suffered a drop in valuation from USD 22 Billion to USD 3 Billion within a span of just 1 year[28].

Byju's failed to file its financial accounts on time, skipped an interest payment on its term loan, and triggered a legal fight with its creditors. Several US-based investors accused Byju's of hiding half a Billion dollars, prompting lawsuits.

Concerns raised by Investors include delayed hiring of a chief financial officer for years, acquisitions of more than a dozen companies across the world, significant employee exits, Board member resignations and increasingly empty classrooms. A major red flag was the delay in filing its financial reports for the financial year ending March 2021 and resignation of the auditor, Deloitte Haskins & Sells citing the firm's unreliable financial records.

This crisis is primarily due to lack of transparency to its Investors, creditors and regulators, which is an important part of good Corporate Governance practices. However, it demonstrates poor management of multiple aspects of ESG: reducing customer engagement, lack of proper governance structure, conflicts with Investors, regulators and auditors and poor business ethics.

28# https://www.ndtv.com/india-news/
byju-valuation-slashed-another-blow-to-byjus-investor-cuts-valuation-by-86-to-3-billion-4620028

It is important to note here that the perceived possibility of a risk on transparency and governance by investors is sufficient to affect their trust in the management and as a result, the market capitalization of the firm.

These case studies underscore the fact that poor performance or perception of poor performance in ESG directly affects the financial performance of the company, irrespective of its size, sector, or geographical location.

Question: What is the role of purpose in this?

Answer: We must begin with the concept of purpose. From there, we establish the appropriate corporate governance structures that will deliver that purpose. This approach is essential to set the organization on a path to success. Only an organization that is set up for success can create consistent, long-term value in the market.

Companies that tend to keep their house in order, fulfilling their purpose, deriving policies from their purpose, having all the policies in place, supported by appropriate governance mechanisms to deliver on those policy objectives are very likely to be successful.

So, how well a company runs itself can tell us what its future is going to be.

Question: Is there a way to identify such companies that are going to be successful in the future? What do they look like? Can you give some examples?

Answer: Look for Companies that have managed to achieve coherence and harmony between their Corporate Governance structure and Corporate Behavior.

To identify such companies, we have to compare and contrast their day-to-day corporate behavior with their Corporate Governance structure.

While the Corporate Governance structure outlines how a company is expected to behave, in theory, corporate behavior shows how a company actually behaves.

When a company wants to achieve certain desired corporate behavior, it aims to do so by designing the Corporate Governance structures to deliver this behavior. However, the actual corporate behavior of a company can be very different from its behavior as desired by its stakeholders.

Ideally, the corporate behavior of a company would be:

1. Consistent with its purpose

2. Consistent with the expectations of its stakeholders and

3. Appropriate in the social context

If a company's corporate behavior deviates from its stated purpose, stakeholder expectations, and broader societal norms, conflicts typically arise. This is found to be true irrespective of the size of the organization or the strength of its brand name.

For example, let's consider Apple.

Case Study: Apple

Apple's vision statement says: "To make the best products on earth and to leave the world better than we found it".

Furthermore, Apple's Core Values mention 'Supplier responsibility' among others. It says that Apple will "hold its suppliers to the highest labor and human rights standards, along with health and safety, and environmental practices."

However, despite this Vision and the Core values that outline the desired Corporate Behavior for Apple, the reality is that its major supplier, Foxconn, continues[31] to be embroiled in a series of worker protests and unrest in its factories that produce Apple's most successful product: the iPhone[32].

This highlights the fact that for even the most successful organizations there can exist a visible difference between their Corporate Governance objectives and the actual Corporate Behavior they exhibit.

Companies that have a gap between their corporate behavior and aspirations as expressed in their vision, mission, purpose, and Corporate Governance structure are likely to face several conflicts. Those that have no gap have achieved complete alignment of their behavior with their Corporate Purpose and Values. These companies are trusted by their investors and other stakeholders in the long run.

31# https://www.npr.org/sections/thetwo-way/2012/02/09/146657989/
protesters-at-apple-stores-demand-ethical-products

32# https://www.bbc.com/news/world-asia-china-63725812

The dichotomy between Corporate Governance Policies and Corporate behavior is a challenge for the Board and the Executive Leadership of the company to address.

Companies that have removed this dichotomy and managed to align their corporate behavior to their vision, mission and policies are likely to transform themselves into Institutions over time. They inherit the trust of their Investors, Society, regulators, and the government for generations. This is a significant competitive advantage, as such companies become irreplaceable and are truly sustainable in the long run.

Question: Are there any real-world examples of such companies?

Answer: The Tata group is one such example.

Case Study: Tata Group

Tata began as a trading company in 1868 in India; however, it is now an Institution that operates across the world. Why is it regarded as an Institution? The Tata group has consistently showcased its commitment to the welfare of its workers, employees, and broader society, even in the absence of a legal requirement to do so. For example, in 1907, even before commencing operations for Tata Iron and Steel company (now Tata Steel), Mr. Jamshedji Tata built a hospital in Sakchi (Jamshedpur) to serve the local community.

While setting up the operations of the Steel company, a simple set of hutments for the steel workers would have been sufficient to house the local workers. However, Jamshedji Tata was fulfilling his vision of building an integrated industrial city, despite there being no such requirement from the government or demands or expectations from the society in India or anywhere in the world[33].

He managed to build India's first integrated industrial city in 1919, complete with all the facilities of a well-planned city: wide streets, parks, schools, hospitals, play areas for football, hockey and areas earmarked for temples, mosques, and churches. Jamshedpur has been ranked highly in quality-of-life indices among cities and is India's most successful, privately run city[34].

Other benefits were offered by Jamshedji Tata more than 100 years ago[35]:

1. Introduced the apprentice system at work.

2. Made available crèches and primary classes for children of women mill workers.

3. Provided free medical help to all employees.

33# https://www.tata.com/newsroom/100-years-jamshedpur-1-tata-steel

34# https://en.wikipedia.org/wiki/Jamshedpur

35# https://www.businesstoday.in/magazine/cover-story/story/tata-steel-history-22810-2011-06-23

4. Provided Gratuity and pension fund, provident fund, maternity benefit allowance and a compensation fund for accidents for all employees.

5. Pioneered the organized flat system of housing.

All these benefits were far ahead of their time anywhere in the world.

No wonder that Mr. Jamshedji Tata is regarded as the 'Father of Indian Industry' and one of the most important builders of the modern Indian economy.

The Tata Group has institutionalized its culture of seeking positive stakeholder impact by setting up a number of Trusts over the years. All these operate under the umbrella of 'Tata Trusts', which holds a two-third stake in Tata Sons, the premier holding company of Tata group of companies.

Over the last 125 years, Tata Trusts have leveraged their unique position as guardians of Tata's capital to make a positive impact on areas such as health, nutrition, education, water, sanitation, livelihoods, social justice, inclusion, skilling, migration, environment, literacy, sports, arts, craft, culture, and disaster management, etc.

This demonstrates the deep commitment of the Tata group and its top leadership to act in the best interests of its stakeholders, not just shareholders. Their efforts extend well beyond the

compliance requirements of the government and certainly exceed any written or expected codes of conduct. Their actions are not only ahead of their time but also deeply aligned with their values.

This demonstrates that it is possible for a company to be 100% aligned with its Purpose, Vision, Mission and Values. In fact, in doing so, a company can build a long-term Sustainable Business that transforms into an Institution in itself over time.

With a combined market cap of USD 300 Billion in Sep 2023[36] across its 29 listed companies, the Tata Group, as a whole, is within the top 25 most valued companies in the world.

Hence, it is possible to do good and be profitable at the same time. In reality, companies that do good not only remain profitable but also achieve sustained success over the long term.

This contrasts with the Fortune 500 list, where approximately half of the companies vanish from the list every 13 years.

Question: Wow, if every company starts to do good for the stakeholders, we will have a prosperous, happy, and harmonious society!

Answer: Absolutely, ESG is indeed based on this simple and practical logic that we can use to create long term value: "Doing well by Doing good"

36# https://en.wikipedia.org/wiki/Tata_Group#:~:text=Established%20in%201868%2C%20it%20is,100%20countries%20across%20six%20continents.&text=There%20are%2029%20publicly%20listed,billion)%20as%20of%20September%202023.

ESG is also multi-disciplinary, bringing in the best of knowledge from multiple fields of study with only one purpose – to provide a framework for companies to be successful in the long run.

"Be the Change you want to see in the World."

-Mahatma Gandhi

Chapter 4

How does ESG Create Value?

What ESG has been demonstrating to us is that financial success is not the starting point. It emerges naturally when we prioritize the wellbeing of all stakeholders. The starting point is to focus on Stakeholder value. Unless the right ingredients are in place, we can't achieve financial success.

ESG encourages companies to pursue 360-degree success with their stakeholders by creating value for customers and employees, strengthening the suppliers, enriching the natural environment, going beyond regulations and being a positive force for the society as a whole. Financial success will naturally follow from this well-rounded approach.

Why? As stakeholders whose lives are being enriched by the company, they will not go anywhere else. They will keep coming back to the company, keeping it relevant for a long period of time.

An example:

Case Study: Unilever

Unilever, an FMCG company that operates in a hyper competitive industry with typically low margins, has been implementing an ESG guided strategy since 2010, called Unilever's 'Sustainable living plan'. As a result, its operating profit has increased consistently, year on year, progressing from 6.4 Billion USD in 2011 to 8.3 Billion USD in 2020 – marking a 30% surge in operating profit over those 10 years, while its total revenues increased only 10% in the same period from 46 Billion USD to 50 Billion USD!

It was a result of their conscious pursuit of ESG, and Sustainability led strategy as chronicled by their CEO, Paul Polman, in his book 'Net positive'.

Hence, ESG is the proverbial horse before the cart. The cart here being consistent financial success.

Case Study: Volkswagen

On the other hand, Volkswagen is another example of a company that prioritized shareholder wealth as its primary objective, even at the cost of harming its stakeholders. However, it ended up harming its shareholders too, as expected.

In 2014, it came to light that Volkswagen knowingly violated the U.S. Clean Air Act. It misled the United States Environmental

Protection Agency (EPA) with inaccurate engine emissions data for its Diesel TDI engines that were in use since 2006.

It had sold approximately 11 million cars worldwide with this flaw for more than 8 years! By 2017, the scandal had cost Volkswagen $33 Billion and landed its top leadership in the US, in jail.

Having learnt the lesson, Volkswagen announced plans to invest $50 Billion for the development of electric cars in 2018. It would have proven significantly more cost effective for Volkswagen's shareholders had the Board and leadership invested in electric cars in 2006, a good 12 years earlier. Had they done so, Volkswagen's shareholders would have avoided a loss of $30 Billion in direct costs of the diesel scandal and unaccounted losses in terms of reputation damage and missed business opportunities caused by their delayed entry into the car revolution within the industry.

Some key lessons:

1. There are no shortcuts on the path to value creation. It is not possible to create consistent, long-term shareholder value by ignoring or harming the stakeholders.

2. On the contrary, Stakeholder capital maximization has proven to be a far superior strategy to maximize shareholder wealth. To be successful, a company needs to aim for stakeholder

capital maximization. Shareholder wealth creation will be a natural outcome of this process.

3. ESG has emerged as a powerful tool in the hands of Boards and Executives to pursue Sustainable value creation for both stakeholders and shareholders. It is not necessary to pick one over the other. In the long run, both go hand in hand.

"Whatever you think or dream you can, begin it. Boldness has genius, magic and power in it"

-Goethe

Chapter 5

ESG vs Corporate Sustainability

Question: So, what do we mean by Corporate Sustainability?

Answer: Before grasping Corporate Sustainability, first we need to understand the broader concept of sustainability. If we break down the term, Sustainability is the 'ability' to 'Sustain'. Sustenance, by definition, implies long term. It implies a way of living that can be supported over a long period of time. It is all about durability and longevity.

It does not occur randomly, it is a result of conscious choices that we make in terms of how we live, and the outcome of those choices is Sustainability – living in balance and harmony, living responsibly. This creates positive results, setting up a positive reinforcement loop, thus enabling us to live in balance and harmony over a long period of time.

It can be used in any context. Whether personal sustainability, or that of companies or that of other organizations or a country or a civilization or this planet.

When used in the context of companies, Sustainability implies making those choices across all its activities, all its operations. Therefore, when used in the corporate context, Sustainability is called 'Corporate Sustainability'.

Question: So, We how does it relate to ESG?

Answer: ESG serves as a lens, a perspective, a 'frame'-'work', a way of looking at a company that allows us to make sustainable choices across those dimensions—environmental interactions and performance, social interactions, and performance there, and governance related interactions and performance there.

Hence, Corporate Sustainability is a goal while ESG is a powerful tool or framework to deliver that goal, that has the backing of Institutional Investors who are interested in the long-term success of the company.

Question: So, is it truly worthwhile investing time and energy in ESG if we are aiming for growth?

Answer: Yes, especially if you want to create, operate, or work in organizations that will thrive over the long term. ESG is a robust framework or tool to deliver long term Sustainability. Sustainability is a goal. ESG is a way to achieve that goal.

Question: Thanks for explaining that.

Answer: Yes, ESG and Sustainability are often used interchangeably but essentially ESG is a framework developed to help the Institutional Investors, so they could identify and invest in companies that are Sustainable in the long run. As a term it originated in the Investment world and grew from there. Corporate Sustainability is a term that originated in the corporate world. However, both are leading to the same goal: high performance, high value, responsible Companies that balance the interests of all their stakeholders equally well.

Need for ESG

Question: What was the need to develop ESG as a framework?

Answer: Traditional investment research since the last century has always focused on financial performance of a company. Criteria like annual earnings, costs, profit, earnings per share, return on investments etc. These criteria only provided limited information on how a company is performing in terms of financial metrics over the past years. When you try to estimate these criteria for the future, it is difficult. Ask any financial analyst who is trying to forecast 'g' - the expected growth rate of a company they are assessing.

ESG research and analysis framework answered that long unfulfilled need of Investors to forecast the company's future performance and earnings with a higher degree of confidence.

Question: How exactly does it answer that need?

Answer: ESG metrics cover operating performance of the company. These operational indicators often serve as leading indicators of a company's future financial performance. For instance, looking at trends in production data and raw material sourcing, we can estimate whether the company has a growing order book or not. Growing order book of today will result in greater sales in the next financial year. Similarly, looking at the hiring trends we can figure out if the company is growing its revenues or not.

Hence, all ESG parameters today tend to give a picture of the financial metrics of tomorrow.

Continuing with this effort, looking at a range of such parameters, we can estimate with a much higher degree of confidence, the future financial performance of the company. This, in turn, proves advantageous to investors. When you put all of these leading metrics together and organize them around three themes: E, S and G, they comprise ESG.

ESG Completes Financial Research

Question: So, this is the leading framework used now in the investment world?

Answer: ESG is not a replacement or substitute for traditional financial research. It supplements financial research,

and most smart Investors use it exactly for that purpose: to get additional information and insight beyond what they can get from financial analysis alone. Combined with financial research, ESG research gives a complete picture of the company: its past performance and likely future performance.

Question: Great to know how ESG grew so much.

Answer: Yes, ESG grew because it caters to an unfulfilled need of Investors. However, it doesn't contradict either traditional financial research or Corporate Sustainability.

Growth History of ESG

The term ESG was coined only in 2004 and gained popularity after 2006 when the non-profit organization 'Principles of Responsible Investment' (UN PRI or PRI, backed by the United Nations) came into existence.

Institutional Investors swiftly enrolled as members of PRI and agreed to integrate ESG principles into their investment process. By March 2023, more than 5391 Institutional Investors became signatories to the UN PRI[37]. These Investors have assets under management exceeding USD 121 Trillion. Hence, this has been the driver for the growth of ESG in the Investment research process.

37# https://www.unpri.org/annual-report-2023

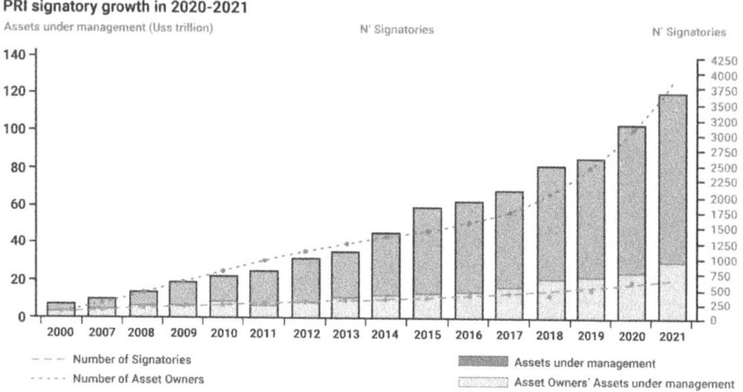

This growth in investor demand has led to the creation of ESG indices and investment funds specifically targeting companies with high ESG scores. Supporting this ESG-focused investment effort was the proliferation of ESG Ratings. Similar to credit ratings, these ESG Ratings are issued by research and data organizations that collect ESG data, perform analysis and issue scores to companies around the world.

Over the last two decades, ESG has grown rapidly, and today, ESG-focused investing is a multi-Trillion-dollar industry.

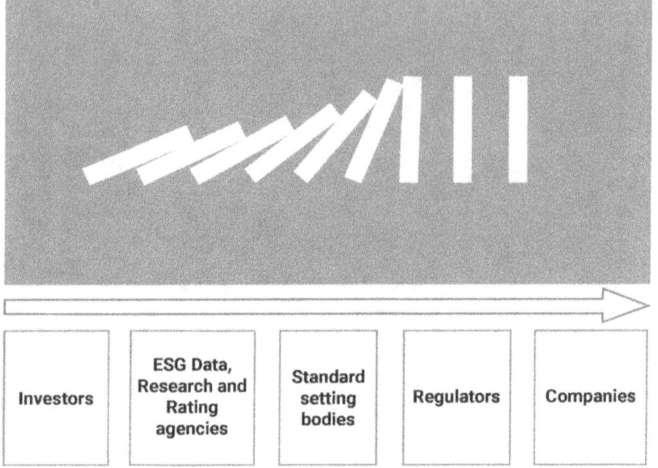

Origin of ESG

Though ESG as a term was officially coined in 2004, the underlying causes driving its growth had been present for a long time. The origins of ESG can be traced back to the 1970s when the inaugural United Nations Conference on the Human Environment was held in Stockholm, Sweden to discuss environmental issues for the first time at a global level, and it resulted in the creation of the UN Environment Program (UNEP).

In 1987, the concept of sustainability was first defined in the Brundtland Report. Sustainability can be referred to as a state of balance between consuming what we need today vs the needs of the future. ESG as a framework or tool can help measure and indicate whether that balance exists or not in the

lens of the various stakeholders who influence or get impacted by business choices. Hence, ESG becomes a tangible structure to realize Sustainability within a company as it becomes a compass, highlighting whether a company is moving towards Sustainability or away from it.

This has been the greatest contribution of ESG: it has made Sustainability tangible and achievable and hence accelerated the progress of companies in becoming Sustainable.

Interestingly, ESG research was initially called 'Extra financial research' in the 1990's as it focused on operating indicators and metrics that go beyond financial data. Research firms that pioneered this 'Extra financial research' included Innovest, Sustainalytics, KLD, EIRIS and others.

In the 1990s, the International Finance Corporation (IFC) developed the Performance Standards on Environmental and Social Sustainability. This was followed by the establishment of various organizations to provide a more rigorous and comprehensive set of frameworks and standards to support ESG analysis. However, ESG analysis is only possible if there is reporting of ESG information from companies.

Investors and regulators expect companies to disclose ESG data with the same precision as financial data. Therefore, ESG reports of companies are expected to be accurate, trustworthy, comparable, and accessible.

To help companies to focus their disclosure efforts, a demand emerged for a reporting framework or a standard.

To respond to this need, several local and regional stakeholders developed disclosure frameworks from their unique point of view.

However, the absence of a clear international coordinated effort leading to a single globally accepted standard has contributed to the proliferation of ESG reporting frameworks and standards over time.

ESG STANDARD

A standard is a set of specific, mandatory, and enforceable requirements for reporting of ESG practices that organizations must comply with.

Examples of ESG Reporting Standards[38]:

- Global Reporting Initiative (GRI)

- Sustainability Accounting Standards Board (SASB)

- Business Responsibility and Sustainability Report (BRSR)

- International Sustainability Standards Board (ISSB)

- European Sustainability Reporting Standard (ESRS)

- ISO 26000

- AA1000

38# Not a comprehensive list, there are more.

GRI: Global Reporting Initiative: The Global Reporting Initiative (GRI) standards were developed in 1997 to provide a globally recognized and standardized framework for sustainability reporting. This initiative was established through collaboration between the Environmentally Responsible Economies (CERES) and the United Nations Environment Program (UNEP).

SASB: Sustainability Accounting Standards Board was established in 2011 to develop industry-specific sustainability accounting standards for publicly traded companies.

ISSB: International Sustainability Standards Board is a new standard-setting board that has developed global sustainability reporting standards. The ISSB was established in 2021 by the International Financial Reporting Standards (IFRS) Foundation, with the primary objective of addressing the increasing demand for a comprehensive framework that would be compatible with existing financial reporting standards. The merger between SASB and ISSB was completed to create a unified global standard for ESG reporting that is compatible with financial reporting standards. The merger combined SASB's industry-specific expertise with ISSB's global reach and support from the IFRS Foundation. The ISSB has been collaborating with other sustainability reporting initiatives to release new standards designed to ensure compatibility and minimize duplication of effort.

ESG FRAMEWORK

A framework refers to a set of guidelines or principles that provide a structure for organizations to assess, manage and report ESG risks and opportunities.

In simple terms, a framework provides guidelines, while a standard sets the requirements.

Some examples of ESG Reporting Frameworks[39]:

- Task Force on Climate-related Financial Disclosures (TCFD)

- Taskforce on Nature-related Financial Disclosures (TNFD)

- Carbon Disclosure Project (CDP)

- Integrated Reporting Framework (IRF)

- Equator Principles

- UN Sustainable Development Goals (SDG's)

- UN Global Compact Principles

- UN Principles for Responsible Investment (PRI)

- UNEP FI Principles for Responsible Banking

- UN Guiding principles on Business and Human Rights

- US Green Building Council LEED

- UN Global Biodiversity Framework

39# Not a comprehensive list, there are more.

ESG reporting standards are becoming more prevalent and investors are increasingly interested in sustainability-related information, hence, many companies are choosing to disclose their ESG performance by adhering to multiple standards.

Many countries also have their own regulations and guidelines for companies to report on their ESG performance. As investors and other stakeholders become increasingly interested in sustainability-related information, it is expected that the use of ESG reporting standards and frameworks will continue to grow.

However, there is still a long way to go in terms of achieving consistent and comparable ESG reporting across the global business community.

It is important for companies, investors, and regulators to work together in order to establish a single, globally accepted standard for ESG reporting, and for companies to invest in the resources and expertise needed to implement these reporting frameworks effectively.

As Large companies are exposed to these reporting requirements, their suppliers are also being included in the reporting commitment as several of these regulations require companies to report on their supply chain or value chain entities. Hence there emerged a need for the entire ecosystem to embark on their ESG reporting journey.

ESG Regulation

The European Union Action Plan on Sustainable Finance has laid the foundation for an array of legislations that have emerged from Europe. These include the EU Non-financial reporting directive, Sustainable Finance Disclosure regulation, Carbon border adjustment mechanism and others. These regulations address both investors and companies.

For example, 50,000 European and 10,000 global companies who are doing business in Europe need to report, starting 2024, their ESG performance as mandated by multiple regulations: CSRD (Corporate Sustainability Reporting Directive), CSDDD (Corporate Sustainability Due Diligence Directive) and others.

The US is not lagging behind. Securities and Exchange Commission (SEC) proposed a new rule that mandates publicly traded companies to disclose information on their ESG policies and performance.

In India, The BRSR standard has emerged as part of a new mandate from the Securities and Exchange Board of India (SEBI). BRSR stands for the Business Responsibility & Sustainability Report. From FY 2022-23, SEBI has made it mandatory for the top 1000 listed companies to submit their BRSR report to the stock exchanges as an integral aspect of their annual report.

Hence, there is a rush now, mandated by regulation, to report on these ESG reporting standards and put in place measurement systems for ongoing monitoring and management.

There is no turning back now in implementing ESG in a fundamental and systematic way across Companies.

Globally, regulators are expecting the same level of maturity from companies on their ESG data and disclosures, as they have with financial data and disclosures.

There is a sense of urgency among the more progressive companies to be ahead of the compliance requirements. It is best to start early. Compliance with such reporting requirements needs structural shifts and even transformation in the way a company runs its operations and sources its data internally and from its stakeholders. Implementing such structural shifts and transformations is a time-consuming effort. Noncompliance has a significant cost – possibility of losing the listing or the reputational risk of being fined.

Why has ESG been Gaining Importance?

To summarize, there are many fundamental reasons for the growth of ESG:

1. Stakeholder demands. The biggest driver is increasing investor demand, as mentioned earlier. Investors who look at an ESG report or ESG rating, in addition to the company's financial

report and credit rating, are better informed about the current and future risks. It is not surprising therefore that investors have been a driving force behind the increasing momentum of ESG. In addition, other stakeholders are also demanding companies disclose their 360-degree impact.

2. Push for corporate reporting. Owing to increasing demand from investors, the adoption of ESG to report corporate performance has been growing. Disclosures have also emerged to be a strong communication and messaging tool for Corporations to convey their commitment and vision to the broader audience.

3. Higher ESG Ratings driving down the cost of capital. Increased investor appetite for ESG analysis has led to the emergence of ESG Rating agencies that assess companies on their ESG performance vis-à-vis their industry counterparts. Similar to credit ratings, Companies that rate high (ex AAA) on ESG ratings get greater access to capital, at a lower cost, and improve their market capitalization as well as reputation. This provides an incentive for companies to disclose more and perform better on ESG over time.

4. Value generation through ESG Performance. ESG has become a Strategic tool for the Board and Top leadership of a company to understand and improve the drivers underpinning its financial performance. The ability to access key drivers of value is a significant enabler for Board and

Top leadership to consistently create value in the longer term. We have seen how companies like Unilever have leveraged ESG as a strategic driver for value creation.

5. ESG Alpha. ESG applied rigorously, correlates well with the company's future financial performance. There has been increasing recognition that several ESG policies and operating indicators are leading metrics of a company's future financial performance. This correlation has further fueled the mainstreaming of ESG in the Investment world.

6. Regulatory push. Given the substantial momentum amassed by ESG over the last 20 years, regulatory bodies in South Africa, Europe, India, Singapore, and the USA have started to pass legislations that demand companies to proactively manage and report their ESG performance. Any company that does not comply with them will not be able to operate in these jurisdictions or list in their capital markets.

Other Applications of ESG

Beyond this perspective, ESG is the only answer we have to respond to the ever-increasing, vast, and diverse challenges that our society is facing – climate change, pollution, biodiversity loss, inequality, poverty and corruption.

ESG as a framework can be applied to a person, a family, an NGO, a company, a city, even a government and a country

or the planet! It can be applied to any human activity. We are only limited by our imagination!

There are some cities around the world which are applying ESG as a framework successfully to plan and deliver services to their residents and other stakeholders. They are called Sustainable smart cities or other similar names.

Question: What are the Goals of UN Sustainable Development (SDG's)?

Answer: In essence, they are the application of ESG as a framework to countries!

The Paris Agreement, the legally binding international treaty on climate change, is a specific application of the ESG framework that relates to greenhouse gas emissions (part of the E pillar of ESG) to the participating countries, to achieve a specific climate goal.

Question: Then why is there so much focus on ESG only for companies or businesses?

Answer: If we apply the 80-20 principle, we will get the greatest value by utilizing ESG to support businesses to become more productive as that is the core engine of economic value creation.

Small, medium, and large businesses can utilize all the capitals available – natural, social and financial, to lead value creation for the society. As a result, businesses have an important role to play in creating a society that is equitable and prosperous for all.

ESG as a framework is a powerful tool to help focus the energy of the business world in moving in that direction!

Chapter 6

Let us Summarize

So, what have we learnt till now?

The adoption of ESG as a framework to analyze companies has grown multi fold, backed by most progressive Institutional Investors. Investors have been asking companies to report ESG performance in addition to financial performance. As a result, Corporate ESG disclosure has experienced a remarkable surge in recent times. This has led to an unprecedented boom for professional services and platforms to help companies fulfill their reporting requirements. Climate change and Net zero targets (part of ESG) and planning have only added to this growing demand.

Additionally, there are companies that have realized the strong business case to use ESG as an engine to create higher profits consistently. These companies have demonstrated that letting ESG drive their innovation agenda across their stakeholder touch points leads to significant operational gains, which eventually translates into consistent growth in profits. Unilever, Tesla, and Tata Group examples demonstrate this.

So, whereas a few decades back the question being asked was: "Is it possible to make money while doing good?", case studies like these have demonstrated beyond doubt that "only by doing good consistently, it is possible to make money in the long run".

ESG has also been applied to the financial services sector it was born in, leading to the development of new areas of practice called Sustainable Investing or Responsible Investing, Sustainable Finance, Sustainable Banking and Sustainable Insurance and other efforts.

Additionally, a greater number of use cases or applications of ESG are emerging in multiple contexts: nonprofits, cities, countries (SDG's), across the planet (Paris climate agreement, Save the oceans etc.). This is leading to an unprecedented demand for people who are expected to have the necessary skills and experience to apply ESG in the respective contexts.

This is leading to a hiring boom in ESG. While other sectors are either growing very slowly or firing people in large numbers, there are a vast number of open positions for ESG across industries. This demand for talent is expected to increase 10 times by the year 2030. Additionally, with Artificial Intelligence

(AI) taking away jobs in several industries, ESG is the perfect answer to that challenge, as it is going to create 'Green jobs' across multiple industries.

It is therefore worth making the effort to either:

- Upskill and transition to an ESG career, or

- Upskill and apply ESG principles into our current role.

Chapter 7

What can we do now?

Question: So how can I develop my ESG expertise?

Answer: Invest in reading, join a community where you can learn together with others, ask questions, seek answers, and start looking at the world from this new perspective.

Most importantly: Implement what you are learning in your work and personal life. Begin by making changes in your personal life first. Once you see results in your life, you will develop conviction, making it easier to implement ESG practices at work.

Become a responsible consumer. Monitor and limit the resources you use. Switch off lights when not in use, limit water consumption, and be mindful of consumption in general. There is enough for all our needs, but not for wastage or our greed.

Make choices that have a positive impact on the environment, support small and local businesses, empower people who don't have income or resources, campaign for causes that matter to you, and become a champion for demanding better governance

from companies and local governments. The more you learn and practice, the greater your expertise and confidence will become!

Question: How can I choose the appropriate sources to use, read, study, and select appropriate programs to upskill?

Answer: Read and learn from all the sources that you come across. However, in your learning process, retain only that which resonates with you. Over time, filter and narrow down your sources to those that make sense to you. The ESG industry is full of people from diverse backgrounds. Most are well meaning and passionate about what they are doing. However, not everyone is.

Hence, there are two risks:

1. People who are just at the surface and don't really know the depth of ESG or how to apply it properly. They might unintentionally distort your perspective by sharing opinions and biases instead of real knowledge that delivers results. Wrong knowledge can cause more harm than ignorance itself. They may think and present themselves as experts, but they are actually not. We can see several people who have 'repositioned' themselves as ESG experts, even though they were doing something very different earlier.

2. People for whom it is just another trend, the next "in-thing" which they would like to take advantage of. Making money

is their primary objective, without paying attention to the value created or the impact made by their efforts. Such people do a dis-service, both to others and to the concept of ESG. They do not put the necessary effort, attention, and dedication because it is just a job for them. Their main focus is to make more money, not to show that ESG is useful. There is nothing wrong in making money as long as it is a legitimate part of a value exchange in which meaningful value has been generated for the other party. The problem is that since this type of people do not care enough, they do not put sufficient attention to implementing ESG well and hence do not get the desired results. This brings a bad name to ESG itself. This is one of the reasons for the criticism of ESG that you come across in several places.

Discern. Go for those sources and people who really care about it.

Beware of those who make grand promises but fail to deliver accordingly. It shows they really don't care about you or ESG.

Lastly, beware of people who like to make things more complicated than they are. People who like to cloak knowledge in very fancy terms with very complex explanations are actually creating barriers to entry. They are doing a dis-service by making knowledge more difficult and inaccessible.

In between two parties, if one understands a topic very well and the other doesn't, it creates an unfair playing field. Therefore, anyone who tries to cloak the simple principles of ESG or Sustainability in complex jargon, is actually creating barriers of entry to discourage you from understanding the concept and applying it yourself. They are, knowingly or unknowingly, creating a monopoly of ESG Elites.

Every field of study and every profession possesses its distinct language. A significant part of such language tends to become technical over time. Doctors, engineers, finance professionals and essentially all fields follow this pattern, with ESG being no exception in this regard.

However, the number of terms in ESG have been continuing to grow, and their range and complexity is considerable at this moment. As ESG grows exponentially in the future, this language complexity will serve as a barrier to entry for new talent. It will also lead to confusion and friction. Hence, we need to consciously choose simplicity. Choose sources that help you understand and overcome this complexity.

Look to create value with what you are learning. If it is not creating value, it is not useful. Apply it, make mistakes, learn, and apply it again.

Avoid people who encourage you to continue using services that you don't need anymore. Avoid dependency that has no end. Instead, go for sources and people who assist you in building your own capability and are then happy to let you run after that. This is the biggest test.

Question: Thanks. How can I apply ESG to my current role in my current job?

Answer: ESG can be applied in all functional roles in a company. You can implement it in your current role itself!

1. **If you are in HR: you can explore ways to create positive value for your employees. It will be worth asking these questions to yourself and colleagues:**

   a. Are the existing HR policies and processes effective?

   b. Are they creating value for the organization?

   c. Can they be improved to create more value?

   d. What would be a road map?

   e. Can you measure those improvements in an internal survey? Can the survey results be monitored and tracked over time?

   f. Can people's performance appraisal in the HR department be tied to the results of this satisfaction survey?

   g. Are you innovating to think about the future of work in your company? In your industry?

   h. Are you comparing and benchmarking compensation?

i. What are the likely trends that are going to affect your employees?

j. Do you have a transactional relationship with your employees or is it long-term and strategic?

These are just a few examples of the kind of Questions one would start asking while applying ESG in the HR function.

2. If you are in Finance, consider the following points:

a. How do you handle financial risk? Is your approach aggressive or defensive?

b. Do you have patient, long-term investors, or are you pressured by short-term investors expecting quarterly reports?

c. Are you investing in the future through R&D and growth strategies, or are you reducing investments to show healthy books?

d. Do you follow industry best practices? Or do you go beyond them?

e. Are your financial strategies and policies fair to suppliers and other stakeholders?

f. Are these strategies making your stakeholders poor or causing them loss? How do you measure this?

g. How do you treat your suppliers? Do you pay them on time? Or do you enjoy credit from them at their expense to fund your cash flow?

Hope that you see the direction in which we need to ask these questions.

3. If you are in Technology, please start thinking about:

a. What role does technology serve in the organization? Only to support transactions or is it strategic?

b. Are you investing in tech to cut jobs in the long run or are you using tech to empower your employee base?

c. Are you investing in future-oriented technologies?

d. How ethical are these technologies or business models associated with them? What is their impact on the target audience in the short and long term? Are you being responsible about the impact your technology is creating on them?

e. Are you building your capabilities to be ready for the future?

f. What are your tech dependencies?

g. How does your tech empower all the stakeholders of the organization, whether internal or external?

h. Or do you pass the burden to your stakeholders to catch up with you? And so on.

4. If you are in Operations, please think about:

a. Are you investing in eco-efficiency?

b. Are you consistently reducing your environmental footprint? Have you observed savings resulting from these efforts? If so, how much and what is the trend?

c. Where are the biggest dependencies and risks?

d. Are you working with your suppliers in a transactional way, pitting them against one another to squeeze the maximum benefits from them? Alternatively, do you view your suppliers' as strategic partners in your future growth story? Are they helping you in creating new products and services through capabilities that you don't have but that they bring to the table?

e. How is the work floor in your operations? Is it a place dreaded by labor? Or do they love to work there? What is the track record concerning health and safety?

f. Can labor and employees suggest ideas for improvement? Are they involved in review of policies and processes to improve operations? How much ownership do they display? Why?

5. If you are in R&D, please think about:

a. What is your track record of research and development?

b. What innovations have been generated? How much of it has been used? And where? What results were produced?

c. What are your investments for the future?

d. How much do you invest in your people to improve their capabilities to create new R&D? Do you collaborate across the industry? Or across other industries?

e. Do you collaborate with research institutes?

f. How do you decide which problems to work on?

g. Do you immerse yourself in the world of your stakeholders to figure out the problems and challenges they face, And so forth?

Seeking New Jobs in ESG

If you would like to pursue a new career or new job opportunities, there are multiple options as well:

1. **Reporting and measurement roles:** Given the significant demands on corporates to measure and report their ESG performance according to local and global standards, along with reporting regulations, there exists a significant need for talent who can work with ESG data and reporting. This includes roles for people with multiple backgrounds: whether with the ability to work with quantitative data or ability to work with communication aspects of reporting. These requirements for such skills span across multiple sectors and industries. Hence, if you have a specific industry background, you can look for roles in this category.

2. **Analysis, Research and Ratings:** As there is greater availability of ESG data and disclosures from companies, there's a mounting demand to process, analyze, and research that data into meaningful insights and eventually convert it into ESG Ratings. The core skill set required revolves around research and analysis. Due to a shortage of talent in this area, these roles come at a premium and one can groom oneself to apply for these roles by developing familiarity with ESG as a framework. Opportunities are available within companies, investment firms, rating agencies, and consulting firms.

3. **Advisory and Value creation roles:** These roles exist at either senior executive level within companies or within consulting firms. Someone with advisory and consulting skills could serve in this capacity. However, a deep understanding of ESG as a risk minimization and value creation framework would be necessary to be able to create meaningful value. The surge in demand for this type of talent mimics the boom seen in IT and Digital Consulting a few years ago.

4. **Deep domain expertise roles.** These roles are tailored to apply ESG within specific sectors like Banking and Financial Services, Mining, and others. Someone with a strong background in a specific sector can upskill and be a good potential candidate for such roles.

5. **Deep Technical expertise roles.** These roles involve going deep in specific areas while applying ESG in its distinct aspects.

   a. For example, GHG emissions accounting would require not only good accounting skills but also knowledge of carbon measurements and estimations for specific industries or across industries.

   b. Life Cycle assessments. This skill set involves doing a technical analysis of materials and energy resources used up by a product or process from cradle to grave (beginning to end of use) or from cradle to cradle (recycling). This requires analytical and quantitative skills.

   c. Environmental impact assessments: This scope requires doing specific assessment of the environmental impact of a project or process or activity on given criteria.

   d. Social impact assessments. This involves evaluating the impact of a particular product, process, operation, company, or brand on specific stakeholders or multiple stakeholders. It incorporates skills to design and execute surveys based on a framework created to gather specific insights.

   e. ESG Due Diligence. Investors are increasingly conducting ESG due diligence on companies before making investments. Larger firms also use ESG DD before they

acquire smaller ones, aiming to identify significant ESG risks and opportunities.

These are illustrative examples of the types of roles / areas of work available across ESG.

According to a recent report conducted jointly by Skills Council for Green Jobs and Sattva Consulting, supported by J.P. Morgan, it was projected that India alone would witness the creation of 35 million direct new green (ESG) jobs by 2047. However, the number of indirect jobs that will be created or upskilled to enable a Just and Safe Climate transition will likely be 3 times higher than that, in excess of 100 million.

Globally, the number of jobs that will need to upskill on ESG and Climate transition is expected to be in the range of 1-1.5 Billion by 2050.

Challenges that lie ahead in the ESG Industry

Where there is unprecedented growth, there are bound to be unforeseen challenges.

Learning and implementing ESG is a transformational journey. Only those who genuinely apply ESG principles will discover positive results. Why? Because any transformational effort demands commitment and patience. Processes, operations, and even the culture of a company or organization needs to be transformed for an organization to really reap the full benefits of ESG.

There are two types of companies that end up resisting this transformation:

1. Those who are obsessed with financial performance and earning numbers from quarter to quarter. They do not have the patience to invest in ESG and instead pick up a few convenient things to sugar coat their reports. Hence, they end up greenwashing.

2. Companies that are so deeply entrenched in their old business models, processes, and culture that they decide not to implement ESG at all. However, they are not conceding defeat. Instead, they leverage their existing networks and financial muscle to campaign and lobby with the government and in the media, building and maintaining a position that ESG is 'woke' or for activists and does not work. This can be seen in the backlash against ESG in the USA. However, this is just a front for those 'old economy' companies who do not want to change and would rather try to stall ESG instead of embracing this new way of doing business.

Question: Thank you very much! There would likely be personal challenges as well, right?

Answer: Yes, certainly. Because it is as much an individual journey as it is our collective one. The more we learn, the more questions we will have. The more we implement, the more clarity we will have. However, there will be certain moments when we face some obstacles, and we won't know what to do.

Question: And if I am in such a moment, can I contact you?

Answer: Yes, absolutely! I would love to continue this dialogue with you and support you as much as possible. I have been going through the same journey and whenever I have had a difficult question or dilemma, I have asked those people whom I trust for help and feedback.

Question: So, how can I contact you?

Answer: If you are applying ESG and facing challenges, or if you are keen to build your ESG expertise and feel that I can support you in your journey, please reach out at: https://www.linkedin.com/in/vipularora5/

However, please note that I will filter out the serious ones from others and will answer only those requests where I see a genuine interest and a sincere effort to learn and apply ESG. Hence, please write to me only if you are absolutely sure you pass this criterion.

Question: That will be wonderful. What else are you doing beyond this book?

Answer: I intend to expand upon the content by sharing more information on technical topics like ESG sub themes, indicators, data points and how to apply them. Perhaps this could be the topic of another book.

Question: Can you share what kind of ESG terms and indicators exist?

Answer: There are more than 500 data points that are used. They are mentioned in the Annexure at the end of this book. However, it would be far too lengthy to explain each one of them here in this book. We can perhaps cover them in another way.

Question: So, how should I proceed?

Answer: Take some time to reflect on what you have read here. See how you can apply it. If you face challenges, reach out for help. You can contact me if you have any further questions.

You can also help by spreading awareness about ESG within your community of family and friends. All of us need to do our bit to make a positive impact using ESG.

Question: With all these efforts would it be possible to address the urgent challenge of Climate Change?

Answer: Absolutely. Climate Change is a solvable problem if everyone participates in taking actions that address the four root causes of Climate Change. These actions are:

- We need to cut down the fossil fuel subsidies.

- We need to phase out fossil fuels completely.

- We need to protect existing trees/forests and plant new trees/regenerate old forests.

- We need to de-carbonize our personal and commercial activities.

Question: Please can you give more detail on these steps?

Answer: Sure.

1. **Fossil Fuel subsidies.** Governments around the world are subsidizing the use of fossil fuels to the extent of 7% of Global GDP approximately, as per IMF[40]. This means, in 2022, USD 7 Trillion of subsidies were given to us to consume fossil fuels! This needs to go to zero at the earliest. How can we pay people to produce Greenhouse gases on the one hand and then try to fight Climate Change on the other? We have to start paying the full economic cost of fossil fuels we consume. First by taking out the subsidies that make it too cheap and secondly, by factoring in the financial costs of harmful externalities (the negative consequences of excess greenhouse gases in financial terms).

2. **Phase out Fossil fuels completely.** This is tougher but is necessary if we are serious about addressing Climate Change. When we know that 75% of Greenhouse gas emissions are produced by Fossil fuels, then it is obvious that any serious attempt to solve for Climate Change must hit at this very

---

40# https://www.imf.org/en/Topics/climate-change/energy-subsidies

important root cause. If we don't address the root cause of a problem, there is no way we can solve it meaningfully. In fact, if we apply the 80-20 rule, the first solution to focus on would be to phase out fossil fuels since the effort there would bring the maximum result of cutting out emissions by 75%! A natural question would be: what do we do to replace them? This needs to be done gradually, that is why we need to 'phase out'. We need to ramp up the alternative renewable sources of energy quickly, ramp down our consumption of energy to what we need as a bare minimum (frugality) and manage this transition well. This approach is termed as Just Transition.

3. **We need to protect existing forests, trees, vegetation and biodiversity and plant new trees, regenerate the lost forests and biospheres.** It is an important part of the solution to the climate crisis. Trees capture carbon dioxide from the atmosphere and store the carbon in their leaves, stems, and roots, eventually increasing the carbon stored in soil. They are one of the sequestration engines of nature. Earth had about 6 Trillion trees[41] historically. However, we have cut down half of them, leaving only about 3 Trillion trees now[42].

41# https://www.plant-for-the-planet.org/Trillion-trees/

42# https://www.science.org/content/article/
earth-home-3-Trillion-trees-half-many-when-human-civilization-arose

More significantly, we have lost entire forests – about 33% of them in the last 10,000 years[43]. A forest is a bigger loss since it is an entire ecosystem including multiple species. We cannot restore all 3 Trillion lost trees, but we can restore up to 1 Trillion trees without encroaching on agricultural land. This is a game changing piece of the solution as 1 Trillion trees would capture anywhere between 25% to 33% of greenhouse gas emissions resulting from human and industrial activity. In fact, if we switch to regenerative farming using the technique of mixed farming, we can restore even more trees.

So, as we phase out fossil fuels, we should simultaneously plant more trees and regenerate forests so the cumulative effects of these two solutions add up, bringing down the cumulative emissions below the critical threshold needed to avoid catastrophic consequences. One important point to bear in mind as we deploy this solution is that we should conserve and replant native and endangered tree species to achieve this objective. There is a reason why Nature chose to locate specific species of trees for a specific climatic region. They are the ones best placed to serve that region.

4. **The last but not the least important piece is: we need to decarbonize personally and in our industrial**

43# Hannah Ritchie (2021) - "The world has lost one-third of its forest, but an end of deforestation is possible" Published online at OurWorldInData.org. Retrieved from: 'https://ourworldindata.org/world-lost-one-third-forests' [Online Resource]

ecosystems. The more careful and frugal we are in our personal life, the more 'responsible' we will be as consumers, the stronger these signals will be picked up by companies. All of this naturally leads companies to invest in de-carbonization of their products, processes, and value chains. In de-carbonization, prevention is better than cure. Every emission avoided is more valuable than an emission released to the air and later sequestered.

Question: So, if we implement these four steps, we will be able to solve the problem of Climate Change?

Answer: This gives us the direction. It is important to understand the root cause of a problem only then we can solve it. Correct diagnosis is key.

Humanity and other species have been living fine on this planet for a long time. Climate Change has appeared as a consequence in recent history, because of a few factors:

1. We have grown 8 times in population in the same 300 years[44].

2. We have industrialized rapidly in the last 300 years using an extractive model of growth without factoring in externalities especially cost to the nature and the environment. We have done this either out of ignorance or greed. Most of this growth has relied on fossil fuels and destruction of forests and natural habitats.

44# https://ourworldindata.org/population-growth

3. This irresponsible production and consumption has been glorified long enough, celebrated through inaccurate measures of progress like GDP, which are linear. We cannot grow in a linear way infinitely, as mentioned in a previous section. Nature works in loops or circles.

4. We have zealously exported this model of irresponsible production and consumption globally, promoting it as the de-facto model of "development".

However, now we can see the limits and consequences of this approach. Climate Change is just one result. Biodiversity loss is another. Social consequences are also there, especially the widening gap between rich and poor. Facts don't lie.

We are living in a civilization that has been built, especially in the last 300 years, at the cost of nature's ecosystem. Nature has been an afterthought for us. However, having understood this now, we need to course correct immediately. We are part of Nature. If we destroy Nature, we will get destroyed along with it. We don't have another planet, only this one.

Who in their right mind, destroys their own home?

<u>The most important fact is that it is STILL possible to course correct,</u> provided we wake up and get into action quickly – individually and collaboratively. It is doable but it requires a rigorous effort of courage and character.

We need to first accept and discuss the truth. Understandably, there are industries and companies that continue to deny the connection between fossil fuels and Climate Change. Why? Because their livelihood depends on it.

However, they are missing the point. Which comes first? Survival or livelihood? The survival of this race and entire ecosystem is at risk if we do not act now.

Here is a Mantra to assess if our work is part of the problem or solution. We should ask this question to ourselves:

"The work that I am doing today, is it making the world a better place. Am I leaving the world a little bit better for my children?"

If we are harming the environment, harming others, or reducing the chances of our survival then is it worth continuing with that work?

Question: Let us say the answer is no. What should we do instead?

Answer: We should change our role definition and work for Solutions. Livelihood is fundamental for all of us. However, instead of doing work that leads to Climate Change and harm of other stakeholders, it would be better that we change our focus to creating Climate Change Solutions.

Solving for Climate change requires new technologies, new processes, new business models and new ways of collaboration.

Majority of the solutions that we will need do not even exist; they need to be created. There is a massive need to invest in R&D and Innovation.

In fact, there is massive economic and ecological opportunity in creating new Climate Change solutions. There is more money to be made there in the New Economy than staying invested in the old economy. By very conservative estimates, there is a minimum of USD 40 Trillion of new opportunity in creating Climate Solutions for the world.

Sounds far-fetched? There are ample examples of this already around us. Take Tesla.

Case Study: Tesla

Tesla was set up in 2004 to make EV cars after General Motors (GM) recalled all its EV1 Electric cars in 2003 and destroyed them. Tesla launched its first EV car in 2008. Despite facing several challenges along the way, Tesla is now the largest producer of EV's globally.

Tesla has a market capitalization of USD 650 Billion, having sold a cumulative 4 million cars globally. This compares with the market capitalization of USD 37 Billion for GM that abandoned a successful EV1 Electric car in 2003.

So why the approx. 20 times difference in market cap? Tesla is expected to grow much faster than GM. It has created a new category and is expected to lead that new category. Market rewards Innovation leading to revenue growth.

Though the EV technology is not perfect, it represents a significant step up from Internal combustion engines that pollute significant amounts of lead, and GHG emissions like CO_2, NOx, SO_2 that not only lead to Climate change but also adverse health effects, particularly concentrated in large cities.

Likewise, there are multiple other solutions needed that will not only benefit the environment but also be economically rewarding for those who do not lose time in pursuing them.

It has become financially imprudent for companies to ignore the traditional externalities of clean air, clean and consistent supply of water and other natural resources and rising income inequality. When consumers have to pay to install air purifiers and water filters to live, companies need to be pro-active in being part of the solution. As Alan Jope, ex CEO of Unilever put it clearly: "Business can choose either to remain part of the problem or to be a contributor to the solution".

Question: Then why do some people continue to criticize the focus on Climate Change or Sustainability or ESG?

Answer: Yes, there are some who continue to challenge the validity of Sustainability and ESG, calling it 'woke' or 'leftist'. The worse is that not only they are discrediting the practitioners or companies serving in ESG and Sustainability sector but also the field itself!

It is ok to criticize specific people or companies or even industries. But it is not OK to criticize an entire field of work. That is inaccurate and exaggerated. We have seen enough data in this book and elsewhere that ESG, Sustainability and Climate Change principles are real. Numbers are speaking very loudly. The Science behind ESG and Sustainability is very strong. It is a different matter that very few people understand it since this is a new field of work.

The science of Climate Change is well established with work of IPCC[45] and other related organizations.

Would you criticize Physics? Do you criticize Physics when a rocket crashes?

No, you set up an inquiry to find out what went wrong, because perhaps a professional made a mistake. Perhaps the space agency or their supplier made a mistake. But the Science never makes mistakes. We may err in implementing it, but the science always works.

Likewise, it is foolish to criticize ESG, Sustainability and Climate Change.

Every industry and every field have their imperfections. ESG, Sustainability and Climate Change industry have their own. But we can talk about this, we can debate it, we can discuss it and

---

45# https://www.ipcc.ch/

try to resolve these. We should not discredit the science behind it. That is going too far!

Question: So, there are challenges in the ESG and Sustainability industry? What are they?

Answer: The truth is that not everything is perfect and well organized in the ESG, Sustainability or Climate Change industry, if we may call it like that. Like any other industry, it has its own challenges. More so since it has been growing rapidly in the last few years.

This rapid growth has led to a significant demand for expertise. But the reality is that we do not have significant supply of expertise in this domain. As a result, we have a large delivery gap.

The challenges posed to a ESG and Sustainability professional are complex and multi-dimensional. Even if one is simply reporting on ESG data, it is not easy to understand the terms and definitions and apply them in multiple contexts or industries. It takes practice, learning and some more practice and some more learning till we get it.

Now when it comes to using ESG/Sustainability to create value - reduce risk for an operation or organization or to create new revenue streams or to improve profitability, then the challenge is even greater. It takes deep expertise to achieve these objectives. One has to know the exact drivers of value. One has

to create a recipe: figure out the ingredients, measure the quantity of each of them, get the timing right, the stakeholders right and work out, like an orchestra that each one collaborates at the right moment, to the right extent and only then a Sustainability/ESG initiative will succeed. Only someone who has done this several times can actually do it with certainty, confidence, and conviction.

There is a shortage of authentic deep expertise in the industry to deliver this kind of value.

Question: Understood. But where is the risk coming from, in executing such deep expertise programs?

Answer: Unfortunately, as it happens in other domains as well, when presented with an opportunity, there are some people who transition quickly and position themselves as 'experts' but when it comes to delivering such depth of solutions, they are unable to deliver.

Most people overestimate their expertise on ESG and underestimate the time, effort and cost it will take to deliver a high-quality robust program. Why? They do not have prior experience having delivered something meaningful.

On the other hand, companies also have misplaced expectations as they consider an ESG or Sustainability initiative as just 'one another' initiative like tech implementation and do not provide sufficient budget or time to execute it. Hence, neither the buyer knows how to estimate the scope well and then how to price it, nor the seller. All of this setting up the stage for failure or unrealized expectations.

Hence, there is a need for the 'expert' to be authentic and bold and set up realistic expectations and for the company to trust the truth when it is told.

This misplaced sense of expertise leads to quality concerns on what has been delivered (either a product or a service) leading to 'Greenwashing' and as a result there is criticism of the industry itself.

Question: So, what can we do about it?

Answer: There is also a perception issue. To some people ESG and Sustainability appears to be easy and generic. Some people assume that they can learn it quickly. Simply by learning the language and terms. This is a grave error. ESG and Sustainability is far deeper than it looks, like an iceberg. There is much more to it, than what we see.

Hence, we need to invest the necessary amount of time and effort to nurture and develop our expertise. Learning the terms and the Language is only the first step. What after that? How are we going to deliver the actual value? This requires much deeper work.

If we have done it before, great. If not, this can only be learnt first by being honest about it and then by doing the actual work, making mistakes, learning from failures, and then doing more work, without giving up. Like with any new discipline. Like when we first learnt to ride a bicycle or to swim. No one learnt it in one go. Honesty, Patience, and Perseverance are needed.

Most important ingredient: to be honest and truthful to ourselves and to others on what is realistic and achievable.

Question: Thanks, this is what we can do as an individual. What about collectively, as an industry?

Answer: We can find decent number of people with 5 years' experience in this sector. However, if you are looking for experts who have been working for more than 20 years it is less than 100 people in the entire world.

Look at any stakeholder segment: whether academic faculty, or investors or industry practitioners or consultants, the reality is that there are not more than 100 experts in total globally who have spent their entire career working in this field and have developed a unique proven solution to solve one of the fundamental challenges of implementing Sustainability and ESG in any domain. So, we need to build capability at an industry level to be able to contribute meaningfully and positively.

Question: Oh, I thought there were far more.

Answer: Simply because Sustainability as a field was not a popular and lucrative career option 20-30 years ago.

Why? because Technology or IT was booming, there was more money there. Most smart talent was either in technology or entering IT. Those who could, were either working in financial services or Investment banking or other fields like medicine, accounting, legal etc. These are the professions that were paying the most in the last 30 years. Sustainability career was never a lucrative career till recently.

Question: So, what changed?

Answer: The covid pandemic changed this to a certain extent. Lot of professionals around the world switched or began their switch to Sustainability, ESG and Climate as a career in this period. This is a great sign of progress. However, we need lot more people to develop skills in this area. Either switch full time or integrate ESG, Sustainability and Climate considerations into their current roles. This is what we need.

And we need lot of upskilling, cross skilling, debate, conversation, cross learning etc. All the typical activities that characterize the beginning of an industry need to happen. Only they need to happen in a much shorter time frame. Because we do not have the luxury of time that we had in other industries.

This book is an attempt precisely to reduce the experience gap by sharing learnings so that everyone wins by using them. There are others who have been doing their part. I learnt exactly like this, gaining from others before me and I am doing the same, 'paying it forward' to the next generation.

Let us collaborate on this capacity building effort.

My ESG Journey

My interest in Sustainability ignited in 1997, when I was in the 3rd year of Engineering at TIT Bhiwani. I had come across the article 'Beyond Greening: Strategies for a Sustainable world' from Prof. Stuart Hart in the Harvard Business Review. For an entire month, I could not sleep well. I was moved by the challenges our world would face - resource shortages, lack of food for all, increasing pollution, biodiversity loss, and climate change.

However, I thought to myself, what can a 3rd year college student do about global challenges?

I graduated in 1998 and joined a job that I had secured from campus placement. Despite achieving success and earning a promotion within a few months, concerns about Sustainability continued to bother me. Consequently, I left that job and joined Lokayan, an NGO based in New Delhi, India at half the salary. My project called "Seeds of Hope" focused on documenting examples of Sustainable living across India, with the intention of presenting them to the Planning Commission (now Niti Ayog) of the Govt. of India so that they could be scaled up.

Although, I enjoyed the work, I could not see how it was going to be scaled up in my lifetime. On December 29, 1999, I contacted Prof. Stuart Hart and asked him to guide me as I wanted to build a career in Sustainability. He responded on 4 January, 2000 saying, "This is the best email I have received to start the new millenium!". He advised me to pursue an MBA and enter the business world, noting that effecting change through the business sector was the most efficient route to creating a sustainable world.

I followed his advice and joined the next MBA program at TAPMI. During my MBA studies and the subsequent job positions, while I could not fully implement Sustainability, I tried to implement as much as possible in the guise of Business Process Reengineering. This quick fix worked for some time, and I was at peace. As a bonus I had the privilege of meeting Prof. Hart during one of my work visits to the USA in 2002. From that moment, we became friends for life. I have called him "Stu" since then.

However, in 2004, when I was awarded a fellowship at Stanford University to apply IT for Sustainable development and solve real-world problems, I could not restrain my enthusiasm and started to look for opportunities to implement real Sustainability proactively.

I tried to transform India's agricultural market by creating an online agricultural exchange, where farmers could trade online and sell their produce, helping them double their income, while removing food wastage from the supply chain. Although, this venture met significant success initially, it could not be continued due to reasons that were out of my control. I had to get back to the drawing board.

Next, I aspired to launch a marketplace like eBay or Amazon to sell Sustainability rated products and services. However, this concept required significant funding, and no one I met in Silicon Valley in 2006 was ready to invest in it. Surprisingly, the tide turned when Al Gore published his documentary "An Inconvenient truth" and suddenly global warming and Sustainability became popular. But by then, I had already returned to India and was on to something new.

Dr. Matthew Kiernan and Pierre Trevet from Innovest advised that instead of trying to rate products and services for Sustainability, it was better to rate companies. Their logic was that data was not available for product level ratings. It took me one year to accept this compromise, and eventually, I agreed to work with them to start rating companies in emerging markets where they needed help to expand Innovest's coverage.

My wife and I started Solaron in 2007, with a humble team of 15 analysts whom we hired at coffee shop interviews in

Bangalore. It was a time when no one in India was talking about ESG. During the interview, each of the analysts asked us what the work was about, and we tried to explain to them (to the best of our ability) that it constituted a subset of investment research and analysis, but something that they would learn and apply on the job.

Grateful for their trust as well as Innovest's support, we started our journey on ESG Ratings. Later our team of analysts expanded to 85, and they were all locally situated within the 15 emerging market countries we covered.

From 2010-11, in the background of global crises like Enron, Worldcom, MCI, Satyam, BP oil spill and Sub-prime mortgage crises, when questions were being asked about the lack of early warning insights provided by ESG Ratings, we realized the damage corporate greenwashing and lack of rigor in data collection, analysis and research methodology in the rating process was causing to Investors.

In this piece "Madness in markets: Coming soon to an Emerging Market near you" published in Institutional Investor magazine in 2010, we called upon the need to do deeper research and validation in the ESG Rating methodology:

https://www.institutionalinvestor.com/
article/2btgcm3sl4fnpmfubhgcg/portfolio/
madness-in-markets-coming-soon-to-an-emerging-market-
near-you

Reinforced by the realization that conventional models of ESG ratings were particularly ineffective in assessing EM companies, we created the world's first Emerging market ESG ratings framework "Best in Context" back in 2010.

This pathbreaking framework was based upon the importance of local context in assessing EM companies. Most global rating firms assessed EM companies in the same manner as those in developed markets, creating a distorted view of their performance.

The results of using this methodology were exceptional: the methodology was able to successfully highlight risks ahead of time. It predicted the USD 20 Billion Corporate Governance scandal at Petrobras in 2012, 2 years ahead of time before it surfaced in 2014:

https://www.youtube.com/watch?v=J0U2Sn9DrlU

The methodology was consistently predicting risks ahead of time, from 2011 to 2018, not only in EM's but also in global firms. This led to Global Institutional Investors of the likes of Blackrock, BMO Global, Aviva, CalPERS, Swedish Pension Funds and Nordea to seek our inputs on ESG Ratings of their portfolio companies. By 2014, USD 13 Trillion of Global Investors had signed up to use this methodology.

From 2014 – 2018, the "Best in Context" methodology was awarded the #1 rank as the Most Innovative methodology in the industry in Global Industry surveys. Solaron was ranked as

the #1 EM ESG firm for 5 consecutive years. In 2018, Vipul was ranked among the top 25 people who made the most positive contribution to ESG globally, in the survey 'Independent Research in Responsible Investing' of 2000+ Institutional Investors done by Thomson Extel-SRI Connect.

We were doing path breaking work in emerging markets ESG, bringing Global Investors to understand risks in global supply chains better and also conduct site visits in remote supply chains in India, Pakistan, Bangladesh, Africa, Brazil, Peru, Chile, more.

Eventually, in 2018, Solaron was acquired by Sustainalytics, one of the top two ESG rating firms globally. All of our team members became part of Sustainalytics. Between 2007 and 2018, we onboarded a total of 150 analysts, and trained them on ESG. Many of these analysts have since become research specialists, leading teams of multiple analysts, overseeing operations, or managing business units. Some of them went to other careers.

I feel happy that we could support several people in remote locations to take the plunge and transition to ESG. Here, they not only found improved working conditions but also fulfillment in their roles. And as an added bonus, we made some new friends!

Gratitude

These are the people who are responsible for powering my journey

First and foremost, I extend my gratitude to my parents, Sh. J K Arora and Smt. Pushpa Arora, for having faith in me and making tremendous sacrifices to invest in my education and allowing me to pursue my adventures, especially of a career in Sustainability and ESG, even though they did not know what it was, at that time.

While most parents go above and beyond for their children, my parents' dedication has been extraordinary. It was common in our small business-oriented hometown of Karnal (Haryana, India) for boys to join their family business. However, my parents made a huge sacrifice by continuing to invest in higher learning for me and my brother. They knew that this path would take us away from them in pursuit of jobs and career. They chose our success at the cost of their loneliness. Some parents try to keep at least one child with them, but our parents allowed both of us to explore the world. Their contribution is fundamental to my ESG journey.

I am thankful to my brother, Manish Arora, for not only being a good friend and companion but also for helping me to understand the value of good friendship. I have also learnt the values of courage and boldness from him. He has helped me along my journey by challenging me to apply the ESG principles in my own life. This is core.

I am grateful to my wife, Sonali Arora, for always supporting me in my initiatives and being a constant source of inspiration and cheerfulness. Like any wife would do, she challenges me to live what I believe in and talk about, but more importantly, she has been a pillar of warmth and encouragement during the most arduous moments of this journey. This has kept me going. She was also the co-founder of Solaron and shouldered a heavy load, far more than what she had initially bargained for, in those 11 marathon years of building it. Many people told us that it was too risky for us to be doing a startup together, as husband and wife. I give her all the credit for ensuring we not only survived it but came out stronger together.

She has also reviewed this content multiple times as it moved from being a draft to a finished book. Equally, I am grateful to Leela Prabhu, my mother-in-law, for her patience and support during our multi-year adventure in sustainability and ESG. It takes a lot of faith to support something you don't fully understand, and she has been supportive of me and my wife throughout.

My gratitude extends to my mentor and friend, Stu. (Prof Stuart Hart), for inspiring me to begin my Sustainability/ESG journey. His constant feedback, guidance, and advice have been invaluable on this path. For all the accomplishments of Stu, it is surprising how humble and approachable he is! True hallmark of a genius and a source of constant inspiration. He is truly a pioneer and founding father of Corporate Sustainability, having begun working in this field in the 1970s in the USA.

My appreciation also goes out to a host of people including Dr. Matthew Kiernan, Pierre Trevet, Nick Robins, Hewson Baltzell, Michael Jantzi, Hugh Wheelan, Tony Hay, Nagaraja (Naga) Prakasam, Sunil Rana, Christopher Fordham, James Gifford, Kris Douma, Narina Mnatsakanian, Anatoli Van der Krans, Andrew (Andy) White, Mirza Baig, Sasja Beslik, Antti Savilakso, Chad Spitler, Philippe Spicher, Bob Mann, Donald McDonald, Drew Buckley, Mark Tulay, Jerome Tagger, Dr. Raj Thamotheram, Matt Christenson, Bozena Jankowska, Faryda Lindeman, Yann Gerain, Sébastien Thévoux-Chabuel, Sudip Hazra, Kevin Bourne, David Harris, Alexis Cheang, Vicky Bakshi, Juan Salazar, Erik Breen, Rob Lake, Fiona Reynolds, Valeria Piana, Anastasia Guha, Asha Mehta, Diederik Timmer, (late) Valéry Lucas-Leclin, Hans-Ulrich Beck, Vikram Pappula, Megan Wallingford, Catalina Secreteanu, Rachel Birenbaum, Lauren Compere, Priti Shokeen, Laura Nishikawa, Greg Larkin, Dan

Moran and many other friends and colleagues. They have not only been fellow travelers in this ESG journey but also a source of learning, brainstorming, feedback, and inspiration. If I were to name them all, it would run into many pages.

What is common among all of them? They are the pioneers and leaders who have helped create the ESG industry among Institutional Investors. They are the path breakers who, fueled by their passion, continued to persevere in this field of ESG, despite several challenges. Its growth owes much to the collective efforts of these individuals and many more mentioned in this section.

A very special thanks to all the team members with whom I worked at Solaron and that we built together: Sonali Arora, Jayaprakash Mallikarjun, Sauravh Dubey, Amalia Stancu, Irina Burcea, Dumitru Popescu, Cristina Isabela Popescu, Catalin Popescu, Radhika Mehrotra, Manjula Trigunait, Tilianna Zecca, Sumit Saini, Atul Rawal, Mansi Gupta, Pavithra Gupta, Prasanth Nandakumar, Priyanka Joseph, Renu Vasanth Kumar, Sandhya Menon, Shobhitha Unikkat, Vaishali Shah, Shravan Kumar, Vishal Shah, Aiswarya Sankar, Akanksha Babbar, Ashamdeep Kaur, Molly Priya McClurg, Helen Sjolund, Nagendra Reddy, Neethu Roy, Srobon, Chandni, Neha Lath, Nipun Jain, Rakesh Sasidharan, Rohit Jan, Rohit Mukherjee, Alfred Satheesan, Suhas BA, Jyoti Mahajan, K Sri Harsha, Manish Arora, Dan Marius Sorin, Valentin Dumitru, Remus-Alexandru Vatasescu, Macavei Cristina, Jennifer

Márquez, Iuliana Ghita, Ionel Bratu, Daniela Nistoroiu, Radu Apreutesei, Lavinia Bobici, Ela Vasvary, Nicoleta Goia, Ionut Feldrihan, Alexandru Barna and many others.

Likewise, I am grateful to the support from my colleagues at Sattva Consulting: Krishna, Rathish, Aarti, Shrutee Ganguly, Shruti Bharath, Vrunda, Nidhi, Meesha, Sahana, Arushi, Rukmini, Vijay and Jayachandre who gave me feedback and encouragement to complete this book.

Thanks are due to my friends at Landmark Education: Ferdi Dsouza, Vivek Chopra, Sangeeta Chopra, Jay Merchant, Lalit Khorana, Venkataprasad Baddipudi and others. Thanks to Abhishek Kumar and Praj Ashtekar for encouraging me to write this book. Thanks to Rohit Koshy, Harish Agrawal, Manish Gupta and Anuj Mittal for being there to support the beginning of my journey in Sustainability. Thanks, are also due to (late) Smitu Kothari (Lokayan), (late) R K Pachauri (TERI), (late) Anil Agarwal (Centre for Science and Environment) for supporting my quest in early days.

On a personal note, throughout my years of research, I have gained significant insights from the vast knowledge left behind by Dr. Samael Aun Weor, whom I affectionately call a Master. He has done a masterly work of researching and synthesizing the fundamental principles that were responsible for helping ancient civilizations achieve their glory at the time of their peak.

In a lifetime dedicated to this painstaking research, he carved out these principles and highlighted that indeed they are universal and common. Every time someone has managed to use them, they have brought success and good results.

He wrote 60 books on Anthropology and recorded more than 500 audio lectures from 1917 to 1977, a time when there were very limited facilities to do so. Not only that, but he also renounced all the copyrights of his work so that it could be available and accessible equally to all humanity for everyone's benefit, whether rich or poor. This is the true hallmark of a great soul, a Mahatma who lived his life for the benefit of humanity. I consider him to be a true Guru and guide of humanity.

Another Mahatma who has continued the legacy of Master Samael Aun Weor is Master Kwen Khan Khu, who has continued to expand on the works of Master Samael and explained it further by conducting further research. He has also translated all the works of Master Samael into multiple languages, again for the benefit of humanity, keeping it accessible and affordable for everyone. The principle of inclusion being clearly visible in these actions. Another lived example of Sustainability.

The principles of Anthropology are time-tested and, hence, sustainable. Learning from the experiences of ancient civilizations and identifying how they used to live sustainably helps us see that it has always been possible and gives us hope that we can do it too. This has been a great source of inspiration for me.

And last but not least, a special thanks to Akshar Yadav, whom I affectionately call the Godfather of Marketing. The truth is, I learned more about marketing from him than in my MBA program. While my MBA teachers did a great job, Akshar has figured out something about marketing that not many have. Special thanks to Dinesh Verma, Mamta, and Kanishka, the publishers of this book, who have shown a lot of patience with me as this is the first book I have published. Without their help, encouragement, and valuable book-writing tips, I would never have taken 'the plunge.' Kudos to them!

As this is my first book, I invite your feedback. Your insights will help me improve it further.

Let us stay in touch!

If you'd like to stay in touch after reading this book, please feel free to reach out to me at:

https://www.linkedin.com/in/vipularora5/

From Doubt to Action:
A Poetic Journey of
Empowerment

"Our deepest fear is not that we are inadequate.

Our deepest fear is that we are powerful beyond measure.

It is our light, not our darkness that most frightens us.

We ask ourselves, 'Who am I to be brilliant, gorgeous, talented, fabulous?'

Actually, who are you not to be?

You are a child of God.

Your playing small does not serve the world.

There is nothing enlightened about shrinking so that other people won't feel insecure around you.

We are all meant to shine, as children do.

We were born to make manifest the glory of God that is within us.

It's not just in some of us; it's in everyone.

And as we let our own light shine, we unconsciously give other people permission to do the same.

As we are liberated from our own fear, our presence automatically liberates others."

-Marianne Williamson, A Return to Love:
Reflections on the Principles of
"A Course in Miracles"

Annexure

ESG Sub themes and Indicators: only an illustrative list.

This is being shared here to help you think about the breadth of topics one needs to work with, while applying ESG in an organization. However, there is no need to get overwhelmed. Not everything needs to be done immediately. There is a science and art in applying ESG across the organization. More details about this in the future.

The theme of Environment includes a range of sub themes, including:

1. **Environmental strategy and policy**

   a. Organizational structure for environmental strategy

   b. Environment management system

   c. Integration of Environment into core business

   d. Organizational and Board structure for Environment

   e. Executive role linked to Environment management

   f. Compensation linked to Environmental performance

   g. Learning and development

   h. Product Life cycle analysis

    i.   Reporting, accounting, transparency and audits

    j.   Environmental performance standards and certificates

    k.   Environmental Innovation and R&D for process, technology and business models

    l.   Environmental new business development opportunities

    m. Environmental new products and services

2. Pollution

    a.   Direct and indirect land contamination

    b.   Amount of air pollution

    c.   Amount of wastewater discharged

    d.   Impact on Biodiversity

3. Materials used and recycled

    a.   Number of materials used, reused, recycled

    b.   Materials use efficiency

    c.   % Sustainable materials used

    d.   Waste management

        i.   Amount of waste produced

        ii. Waste intensity

        iii. Non-Hazardous waste

        iv. Hazardous waste

        v.   Amount of waste recycled

        vi. Spills

4. Energy efficiency

a. Amount of energy used

b. Energy intensity

c. % energy used from renewable sources

d. Energy conservation targets

e. Energy efficient technologies and processes

5. Water used and recycled

a. Amount of water used

b. Amount of wastewater discharged

c. Amount of wastewater recycled

d. Water use intensity

e. Chemical oxygen demand

f. Biological oxygen demand

g. Total suspended solids

6. Climate Change

a. Climate Change Strategy and Policy

b. Organizational and Board structure for Climate Change Management

c. Carbon Management system

d. Climate performance reporting and monitoring

e. Greenhouse gas emissions

    i. Direct GHG emissions (Scope 1)

    ii. Indirect GHG emissions

- Scope 2

- Scope 3

f. Energy efficiency

g. Supply chain policies and management systems related to greenhouse gas emissions.

h. Net Zero target

i. Road map to achieve Net Zero target

j. Net Zero transition reporting, monitoring and management

k. Climate solutions and new business development opportunities

l. Innovation and R&D in Climate related solutions and new business opportunities

7. Product life cycle performance

a. Measuring life cycle impact

b. Designing for circularity

c. Sustainable Product life cycle design

d. R&D efforts and results

e. Innovation in technology, processes and business models

The theme of Social includes a range of sub themes from:

1. **Human Capital:**

    a. Human capital strategy and policy

    b. Human capital management system

    c. Organizational structure

    d. Recruitment approach and process

    e. Compensation and Benefits

    f. Health and safety

    g. Working conditions

    h. Employability, Training and Development

    i. Performance assessment and monitoring system

    j. Career development

    k. Full time staff versus contract labor

    l. Attrition and retention rates

    m. Succession planning

    n. Board and Executive Committee structure for Human Capital

    o. Employee Satisfaction survey and monitoring

    p. Human capital reporting and accounting

    q. Human capital audit

r.   Human rights strategy and policy

s.   Fundamental human rights at work

t.   Freedom to associate and collective bargaining

u.   Equal opportunity and diversity

v.   Child and forced labor

w.   Labor relations

x.   Employee engagement

y.   Whistleblower policy and mechanism

2. Customer Capital management:

a.   Customer strategy and policy

b.   Customer satisfaction

c.   Organizational structure for Customer capital management

d.   Executive and Board committee oversight on Customer capital management

e.   Compensation linked to performance

f.   Customer engagement

g.   Customer performance monitoring and audit

h.   Training and Development on Customer relations

i.   Product safety

j.   Product recalls

k. Product certification and labeling

l. Service monitoring

m. Responsible media and advertising

n. Consumer protection

o. Customer engagement for new product and service development

3. **Supplier Capital management**

a. Supply chain management strategy and policy

b. Supply chain management system

c. Code of conduct

d. Supply chain audit

e. Supply chain performance measurement and reporting

f. Transparency and disclosures

g. Integration of ESG in supply chain

h. Human rights in the supply chain

i. Organizational structure for Supply chain management

j. Executive and Board committee oversight on Supply chain performance

k. Supply chain initiatives

l. Capability and capacity building in the supply chain

m. Supply chain partnerships

4. Social impact of products and services:

a. Relevant products and services for society

b. Accessible products and services

c. Social impact of products and services

d. Reporting of impact to stakeholders

e. Mitigate negative impact of a product or service

f. Measures for consumer protection

g. R&D budget to develop products for underserved population

h. Support fair market conditions to provide consumers with greater choice at lower prices.

i. Inclusive pricing policy to make products available to underserved population

j. Consumer education on the environmental, social and economic impacts of consumer choice, and promoting sustainable consumption patterns.

k. Consumer policy to promote sustainable consumption patterns

l. Transparency, Reporting and disclosure of accurate information about the environmental, social and economic impact or use of products and services (e.g. product profiles, CSR reports, information centers and

hotlines on efficient use of materials, energy and water, voluntary and transparent labeling programs).

m. Promoting the development/ use of national and international environmental, health & safety standards for products & services

n. Ethics in marketing and communications, avoiding misleading claims

o. Research and development of new environmentally sound products and services and new technologies.

p. Internalize environmental costs.

5. Impact on Society and local communities:

a. Corporate Social Responsibility (CSR) strategy and policy

b. CSR impact measurement, transparency and reporting

c. CSR audit

d. Community engagement strategy and policy

e. Community engagement performance monitoring and reporting

f. Capacity building of local community

g. Creating local value chain

h. Investing in the infrastructures within the local community

i. Local sourcing where possible

j. Understanding the indirect economic impacts

k. Facilitating partnerships

l. Participating in governmental or private programs aimed at developing workers local skills (vocational education and tutorial for production and services skills).

m. Promoting employment and training of local communities.

n. Social inclusion by increasing opportunities for employment and role of minorities, women, people with disabilities, low wages.

o. Offering wages above the minimum.

The theme of Governance includes a range of sub themes from:

1. Corporate Governance Structure:

a. Organizational structure and hierarchy.

b. Board composition and accountability.

   i. Diversity

   ii. % of Non-Executive Directors

c. Executive team roles and responsibilities, capabilities, and expertise.

d. Relationship between the Board and Executive team.

e. Organizational and Board structure for ESG

f. Integration of ESG strategy with core business

g. ESG performance linked compensation

h. Executive leadership and management structure for Sustainability

i. ESG risk management system

j. ESG audit

k. ESG initiatives and partnerships

l. Corporate Governance strategy, policies and incentives

   i. Remuneration policy

   ii. Diversity and inclusion policy

   iii. Policy against Bribery and corruption

   iv. Board diversity

   v. Code of conduct and Ethics

   vi. ESG or Sustainability policy and strategy

   vii. Corporate Social Responsibility (CSR) policy

   viii. Risk management

   ix. Supplier management policy

   x. Whistleblower policy

   xi. Shareholder rights policy

   xii. Succession planning policy

   xiii. Charitable contributions policy

   xiv. Political Contributions and lobbying policy

   xv. Voting policy and shareholder voting rights

    m. Monitoring and evaluation of performance

    n. Executive compensation

    o. Reporting, disclosure and transparency

    p. Audit

2. Corporate Governance Behavior:

    a. Political context

    b. Economic

    c. Environmental

    d. Social

    e. Technological

    f. Legal context

    g. Corporate culture

    h. Influence of senior leadership

3. Conflicts or controversies

4. Corporate Purpose

5. Alignment of Corporate performance with Corporate Purpose